MAKE THE MOST OF YOUR LIFE

SHAPE YOUR LEGACY AND CREATE SOMETHING TO LEAVE YOUR MARK FOREVER.

DR. AMIT DAS

To

All my bosses and students who made a difference in my professional career.

"In the free and easily accessible information era, there is no longer a necessity for individuals to overload their heads with knowledge. The war may be lost by those who regurgitate; those who innovate will plough their own path and triumph. Beacuase there is a clear distinction between winners and losers. Losers give up at the drop of a hat, whereas winners spend time persevering through difficulties. Don't give up, because if you do, you've already lost. In the end, you have no right to complain to anybody about anything if you're not prepared to stand up for yourself. Hence, living in complaint is not worth it. Utilise it to the fullest. Your final day is unknown to you. Live your life to the fullest, in whatever way you see fit."

- Dr. Amit Das, Motivational Speaker, Leadership Coach and Mentor.

Contents

Foreword

"The purpose of life, after all, is to live it, to taste experience to the utmost, to reach out eagerly and without fear for newer and richer experience." – Eleanor Roosevelt

Living your life to the fullest.

Dear Reader,

Thank you for taking the time to learn more about how to make the most of your life and the rewarding outcome of increasing your personal productivity. The only way you think that will define how best you have created your legacy in this life, regardless of where you are from, how educated you are, or the situations you find yourself in. This book, " Make The Most Of Your Life," will make you question your ability to live your life to the fullest, achieve your goals, and have a fulfilling life. You'll realise that all really successful individuals could make it in their lives and leave their footprints after reading this book.

The author will demonstrate to you how you may start to influence the world by altering the way you feel, think, speak, and act. Instead of merely existing, begin to grow! He covers many aspects including the human condition, discovering one's purpose in life, and the secret to long-lasting happiness. He takes us on a memorable trip with his priceless insights on these aspects of life, whether you're wanting to improve your relationships, realise your full potential, learn how to succeed at business, or even how you may give back to the world. He is one of the most well-known and in-demand mentor and life coach in India, having taught thousands of people. This book, " Make The

Most Of Your Life," his passionate creation, distils his life experiences and teachings into a humorous, thought-provoking book that will assist you in aligning yourself with the life you desire.

"The key is in not spending time, but in investing it." –
Stephen R. Covey

This book will provide you with detailed instructions on how to discover the meaning and purpose of your life in order to feel fulfilled and like you're on the right track. Your life will essentially become more useful to you, the people around you, and eventually the world, if you have a feeling of purpose and meaning in it. Dr. Amit Das gave a step-by-step guide for identifying and fulfilling your life's mission.

This book will assist you in understanding such concerns and reprogramming your daily life to produce more uplifting results. Dr. Amit Das sought out these solutions and invested many hours in his quest to improve himself; this book is a condensed version of such transformative encounters and ideas. You'll be helped by this book. In these uncertain times, do you wish someone could just tell you what to do and how to live your life? So the hunt is over right here. This book provides readers with useful "guidelines" that they may immediately put into practise in their daily lives.

The goal of this book is to encourage each reader to create their own legacy. Most people have the desire to pursue immortality. It inspires many people to start families, publish novels, compose music, create inventions, amass cash, or succeed in a myriad of professions. Even within your own family, immortality, or merely being remembered by future generations, is difficult to attain. Many of us experience this inner conflict of feeling aimless and unimportant. Many of us just float through life doing jobs we don't like while accruing massive amounts of debt from college loans and pursuing things we aren't particularly interested in. We completely stop caring about the things that really make us feel alive.

The author of this book tells us a surprising truth about what motivates us. He lists purpose, along with esteem and contentment, as the three main components of human motivation. According to the author, this type of motivation is superior to conventional theories of motivation, which focus on rewards and the threat of punishment.

You'll specifically gain more confidence around others thanks to the advice in this book. It will assist you in modifying and improving any ideas and feelings that may be preventing you from engaging with others in the greatest way possible. You'll discover a number of things, including a little-known technique for how to step beyond your comfort zone in a way that most people have never done before—comfortably and safely. You'll discover how to eliminate the imposter syndrome, stop people-pleasing, reduce self-doubt, understand where it actually comes from, how to read people more effectively, overcome the need for acceptance, stop people-pleasing, and much more.

Most people have the desire to pursue immortality. It inspires many people to start families, publish novels, compose music, create inventions, amass cash, or succeed in a myriad of professions. Even within your own family, immortality, or merely being remembered by future generations, is difficult to attain. Few people have ever met all four grandparents or even know anything about them. Generations pass away in a swirl of nothingness. That much is true. However, if you read this book and take bold action to become immortal, you may do so within your family, community, and, for a select few, globally. Everything is subject to your wishes. You may become eternal by reading this little book. And if you want assistance, get in touch with the author of this book.

A book with a stunning design that is packed with motivational sayings and tried-and-true advice on utilising optimism to build a life you love. How can you actually learn to love yourself? How to change unfavourable feelings into favourable ones. Is it possible to have permanent joy? Life coaching expert Dr. Amit Das provides comprehensive solutions to all of these queries in this book. He survived hardship to become a source of inspiration for countless young people, and he now draws on his own experience and intuitive knowledge to motivate you. By altering your thoughts, you may attract wonderful chances into your life and achieve your objectives by using tried-and-true methods. Overcome your fear and go with the flow of the universe; discover your higher purpose and become a role model for others.

Do you fear passing away? Most of us are much more afraid of being alive and not knowing, so probably not. Live each day to the utmost and treat it as though it were your last. It is therefore evident that the book does not support any means of achieving physical immortality rather, it supports immortality in the truest sense—being remembered by countless generations. You can achieve immortality. This book, "Make The Most Of Your Life," which was inspired by personal experience, was born out of the author's long search for a step-by-step process to achieve perfect clarity and purpose in his own life.

This book offers you a tried-and-true method for developing a thorough grasp of who you are, a clear understanding of the purpose and direction you desire for your life, and how to develop into the kind of person you need to be in order to live that way. He outlines the guiding principles of intentional living that will enable you to take charge of your life rather than let it dominate you.

Thank you for taking the time to read this book.

So, happy reading and learning to all my readers.

Carpe diem.

Dr. Amit Das

Motivational Speaker, Leadership Coach, and Mentor.

Preface

"My favorite things in life don't cost any money. It's really clear that the most precious resource we all have is time." –
Steve Jobs

A book to help you unleash your true potential.

I wrote this collection of thoughts with folks who recognise the value of leaving a legacy in mind, but who are unsure of why they are alive or what they should be doing with their life in mind. It is a collection that will inspire both creatives in general and those who have never thought of themselves as creative or as capable of creating something admirable. These concepts should be read and digested as if they were a collection of flashcards. Examine each of these chapters , then choose one. Before attempting another, give it your complete attention. Each chapter comes with some thought-provoking points on its core.

It's crucial for college students, recent grads, and anybody else who either hates their job or needs a change to become a more significant and real version of themselves. Are you already there? Do you understand the meaning of life? Have you figured out your passions and what you love to do? The two concepts that most define and affect the direction of your life are purpose and passion. You get enthused about life when you are passionate. Your purpose illuminates the way ahead and gives you confidence and courage.

Unfortunately, a lot of us spend our whole lives looking for our true calling and interests since they do not come to us naturally. Additionally, there are occasions when they are right in front of your eyes but you fail to see them. Humans are pleasure-seeking creatures, but if you let pleasure dictate how your life unfolds, you'll never discover your passion and purpose. Do you ever feel as though you don't belong where you are? If that occurs to you, you might want to reconsider your decision. By reading this book, you may change the way you think, uncover your passion and purpose, and locate the place where you belong. Your desire to live can be killed by trying to fit in; you may never find a setting where your abilities and skills are valued and embraced. Also, it feels like life is a never-ending battle to please other people. In this book, I will help you to overcome some of your fears; strengthen your mental fortitude; discover your passion and purpose; feel better about yourself; and reframe your life goals.

What would it be like to be unconstrained and to fly above your limitations? What can you do every day to find tranquilly and inner peace? These issues are addressed in this book in a straightforward yet deep manner. This book will alter the way you interact with both yourself and the outside world, regardless of whether this is your first foray into inner space or you have dedicated your whole life to the inward trip. You'll learn what you can do to stop the repetitive thoughts and feelings that are limiting your consciousness. I will demonstrate how the growth of awareness may help you all in the present and let go of upsetting memories and beliefs that prevent you from finding pleasure and self-realisation.

When individuals have a sense of purpose, productivity rises because this fosters job satisfaction and creates an internal drive for excellence that is considerably stronger than monetary rewards or the prospect of punishment. People who have a strong sense of purpose are also more equipped to adjust and recover in the face of a disaster. Any person who is motivated by their work's purpose is better able to stay motivated and actively engaged in it even in the face of adversity than those who are not.

In fact, it's been estimated that a whopping 95% of people are unsure about their life goals. I was inspired when I realised how successful I had been. After seeing the incredible results for myself and realising how it could help others, I was inspired to compile everything into a single, concise book. You are living your life on purpose when you are enthusiastic about it. If you've ever had trouble figuring out your life's passion or purpose, you may have found that it's really challenging to find answers to the question by merely pondering them. This book is organised using a special approach based on simple habit adjustments that make you face your fears, set practical objectives, and start succeeding in every aspect of your life. Don't settle; begin acting now to lead the life you choose. Anyone who is feeling a little lost, uncertain of what they want, or unsure of which way to go should read "Make The Most Of Your Life."

> *"What you do today, or what you did in the past, should not limit what you can accomplish moving forward."*

This book would assist you in addressing and finding solutions to all of life's most important concerns. What are you still holding out for? You can create and sustain it by using the resources you already have. Join me on this adventure to discover what true happiness is. You can create and sustain it by utilising the resources you already have. It's an expensive game that so many of us play to learn by making mistakes, often again. You can only truly achieve success in life by developing self-mastery, which you may do by using the create your legacy tree paradigm. Then, rather than taking years, your own growth will direct you toward the accomplishment of empowering objectives. Your legacy has four primary legs—love, health, freedom, and purpose—can be strengthened and balanced, guiding you toward positive decisions, worthwhile experiences, and satisfying connections. This is not a workbook; rather, it presents the scientifically supported tactics mentioned inside in an interesting, easily comprehensible manner that will inform, amuse, and motivate you. You may have the foresight and self-assurance to build your own prosperous future. Let's start by claiming your very own happiness tree right away!

> *"Life is a game, so play it; life is a challenge, so face it; and life is an opportunity, so seize it."*

In order to inspire and direct readers to want, pursue, and fulfil their earthly purposes—or to strive to yield abundant fruit and be a benefit to almighty, mankind, and all of creation—this book discusses methodical ideas. It aims to instil a lifestyle of purpose in the reader so that, by almighty's grace , they may live by a plan, desire to be productive, and ultimately fulfil the almighty's purpose.

We were all made to provide solutions to the world's numerous problems and challenges and make it a more pleasant and safe place to live. All men must abandon selfish, avaricious, haphazard, fruitless, and evil lifestyles in order to live intentionally and make wise choices regarding our everyday activities in order to produce a lot of fruits.

There are many abilities, spiritual gifts, and skills that may be used to improve the world and bring glory to almighty. Everyone has the ability to solve at least one specific problem for someone, and this should be realised. One is set to be directed, ideally, to discover his or her purpose or at least become highly fruitful by reading "Make The Most Of Your Life." You can now choose by clicking the order button to either transform your life for the better or worse for the foreseeable future compared to doing nothing.

"Life is a wonderful adventure that should be enjoyed to the fullest every day. The fact that life is a wonderful gift does not, however, imply that you always wake up ready to grasp the day."
-Dr. Amit Das

Acknowledgements

At the outset, I will thank my family for supporting me throughout the journey of writing my book and encouraging me to live my dreams; my son has always been instrumental in giving his inspiration to complete the writing of this book. Despite the fact that I am listed as the author of this book, "Make The Most Out Of Your Life" would not have been published if I had depended entirely on my own talents. Creating this book required more than anything—it took a family of dedicated and caring people who were always prepared to lend a hand.

Writing a book while working full-time is no simple task, so I'd want to express my gratitude to my amazing coworkers who act as cheerleaders in equal measure. Thank you, too, to my students and clients for your patience and unflinching support while I worked on this book!

Thank you to everyone who has listened to me argue for doing everything you can to make your life, including your work life, more progressive. I appreciate everyone's assistance throughout the process. This book would not have been possible without each of you having had an impact on my life in some manner.

Lastly, I would like to thank all the people with whom I have been associated. You gave me power. I would like to thank Notion Press for publishing my book. Finally, thank you all for gifting your time to read this book.

I'd want to convey my heartfelt appreciation to the almighty God for bestowing his blessings and being so gracious.

Prologue

CHAPTER ONE

Keep A Legacy-Driven Mindset

"Apart from values and ethics which I have tried to live by, the legacy I would like to leave behind is a very simple one - that I have always stood up for what I consider to be the right thing, and I have tried to be as fair and equitable as I could be."
-Ratan Tata

What do you hope people will remember you for?

"Legacy" is a popular term. Everyone aspires to make their mark and do something that will last a long time. Nobody desires to be overlooked. But how would you like to be recalled? Some people leave legacies they regret leaving behind because they are implicated in cover-ups, engage in scandals, or perhaps just plain let their family down. You don't have to be that. What you do now will decide if it is feasible for you to be remembered in 100 years—and to be remembered favourably. The qualities of humility, nobility, self-sacrifice, and consideration of others provide the best chance of achieving that sort of immortality.

Even if people don't talk about legacies in casual conversation, practically everyone wonders about them on quiet rights. Especially for those of us who have reached milestones in our lives like maturity, middle age, and retirement. Have you ever observed a butterfly undergoing metamorphosis? Its emergence from its cocoon is painful and challenging. You could believe you're helping it by slicing the top of its chrysalis so it can emerge more easily.

"Legacy is not leaving something for people. It's leaving something in people." - Peter Strople

However, if you do that, the butterfly won't have fully formed wings and will be handicapped for the remainder of its life. Metamorphosis requires difficulties and struggles to occur. They are essential for both leaving a legacy and building one. This list of suggestions for starting with developing and building a legacy may be exactly the right step in the right path for you. People continue living regardless of their current circumstances for the fundamental reason that they have a purpose in life. With such a goal, life becomes manageable and even pleasurable. This collection of thoughts is intended for people who see the value of leaving a legacy but are unsure of why they should do so.

"The purpose of life is not to be happy. It is to be useful, to be honorable, to be compassionate, to have it make some difference that you have lived and lived well." - Ralph Waldo Emerson

People from all around the world are becoming more aware of the value of a good person in their society in preserving social ecological balance, preventing serious misconduct, and averting major conflicts. Good behaviour may be much easier to achieve if a person is built on a sense of shared values and purpose, even though it is crucial for him or her to have deterrent measures in place, such as legal procedures and social justice.

"Be as light as a feather and when they reach for you — you will blow right by their grip; you will effortlessly flow to safety." — Bryant McGill

People who act morally not out of concern for negative consequences but rather because it is consistent with their shared values and goals. In conclusion, a strong moral character that fosters success is built on a foundation of shared objectives. People who live in a society that is built on a sense of shared values and purpose do the right thing not out of concern for negative consequences but rather because it is in accordance with those values and purpose.

"If you wanna make the world a better place, take a look at yourself, then make that change." – Michael Jackson

You need to learn more profound information, like: what is the true nature of the being you refer to as "I"? What is the underlying force that has shaped the person reading this right now? What enthuses you and fills you with rapture? These are hints as to what your soul truly values in order to have a meaningful existence. What is most important? What really is important?

> *"It is the duty of the deliberate life to honour that desire and identify what really feeds, what really summons development, as well, and then share that bigger expression of soul with others."*

Living a life with more thoughts. You possess a lofty desire that is desperate to be realised and expressed. You have the capacity to be a source of possibility. You are a source of potential with unbounded potential. Your life will change if you think about these words for the next 30 days. I am aware that you might not perceive yourself the same way I do. I don't just view you as a human reading words on a screen; I see you as a soul. Beyond the self-perceptions you have, I sense your potential.

> *"Many people think that confidence is something that comes with success, but the truth is that confidence is what actually brings about success. Our own minds and egos are where we get our confidence from. Therefore, developing our thinking is the most effective and simple technique to increase our confidence."*

Adversity contains the seeds of success. In any circumstance, we must search for untapped potential. Due to the potential to express a prejudiced perspective, we must refrain from making snap decisions. Have you ever attempted to rush anything and had it crumble on you? Before the light bulb was finally created by Thomas Edison, 10,000 other designs were tried and failed. What must develop in its own timeframe cannot be rushed. Living effortlessly acknowledges collaboration with life's energies. If you have a tendency to move too quickly through life, consider patience as a virtue. What are you losing by moving too quickly? A hamster running on a wheel understands that the harder it runs, the slower it moves toward its destination. Switch to the leisurely road instead of the hamster wheel; everything that needs to happen will automatically do so. Examine the underlying cause if you need to move quickly. What do you want to avoid? If life slows down, what are you frightened of seeing? which you do not have control over? Keep your mind open to fresh perspectives, doors, and experiences that bring in welcome change. People who complain that life is boring reject this aspect of it. Even though it may be obscure to you, your existence in this space-time continuum is proof of your greatness.

Imagine what might happen if your passion and mission coincided!

- *Have you ever thought about your life's purpose?*
- *What do you feel strongly about?*
- *What if you awoke each day with a strong desire to live your life?*
- *Do you ever have feelings of being lost or lacking anything in your life?*
- *Do you ever consider your options for living?*
- *How do you continually bring your best self forward?*
- *Why do individuals succeed sometimes and fail at other times?*
- *What must be prioritised in order to be most effective?*
- *If you had some guidance, would life be simpler?*
- *Do you believe your abilities exceed what your findings indicate?*
- *Do several anxieties weigh you down?*
- *Do they prevent you from leading the greatest life possible?*
- *But what if worrying has some advantages?*

> *"Your mental state, your thoughts, forming wonderful connections with other people, and making wonderful memories are what bring you the most joy."*

The good news is that you can improve your life in a variety of tiny, straightforward ways. Multiple ways to improve your well-being, assist those around you, and offer yourself the opportunity to live your best life. These ideas could be a wonderful place to start, but only you truly know what adjustments in your life need to be made. Unfollow those that make you feel bad. You know, the one on Facebook who never stops moaning, the one on Twitter who is constantly debating you, or the Instagram influencer who is so flawless that it makes you feel awful about yourself? Right this second, unlock your phone, and unfollow them. You are not in need of that.

We all experience fears. Fear of danger, fear of public speaking, and fear of uncertainty all serve to keep us stagnant and stop us from progressing. Recognize that your worries are the compass for progress rather than avoiding them. Address them and go through them. Check out these four reasons to conquer fear. Make the most of your heart, soul, intellect, and body. You must optimise your mental, physical, emotional, and spiritual well-being in order to live your best life.

You are not living your life to the fullest if you are extremely successful, wealthy, socially connected, and spiritually attuned, yet you ignore your physical health. Likewise, in other circumstances where you "shut off" a portion of yourself. You are the only one you can change. Give up expecting others to act a specific way. Focus on changing yourself rather than putting pressure on everyone around you to do the same. This will make you happier and help you have a fuller life. Express your gratitude. Be appreciative of all you have now and will acquire in the future. Express your gratitude Make sure the folks who have impacted you are aware of your thanks. You'll be astonished at the impact a small deed like this can have. They won't know if you don't tell them.

"Life is always about aspiring for better, and if you aspire for the best, chances are you will get that and more."

What do you hope people will remember you for? Since this is such a complex subject, I'll be honest and say that it was much harder than I anticipated to put it into words. This is the type of query that caused me to reflect deeply for a number of hours before writing this piece. But weirdly, it's something that has been on my mind a lot lately after dealing with the deaths of my grandpa only weeks apart. What do I want people to remember me for, then? Well, a number of ideas crossed my head, some surface-level and some rather profound. But as I continued to think and think, there were really just two things that kept coming to me. Two things were very important. I want to be known as a kind and nice person. I want people to remember me for my humanitarianism. I really think that compassion outshines all. Kindness, in my opinion, has the power to change people's lives, mend broken hearts, and unquestionably help others. However, whether or not I am recognised for it, I want to be known as someone who is kind, sympathetic, and helpful rather than just as someone who does these things. Assisting strangers who become friends in achieving their goals; assisting my family in overcoming difficulties and problems; and everything in between.

"Twenty years from now you will be more disappointed by the things you didn't do than by the things you did." –
Mark Twain

Many people pause at some point in their careers to wonder how they might influence others' futures and whether they are leaving a legacy. According to Charles Dickens, "No one who eases another person's suffering is useless in this life." Let's get right to the subject of creating a company legacy! For as long as there have been humans, legacies have played a significant role in society.

According to research, people are more inclined to make long-term-focused judgments when they have benefited from the legacy of a previous generation. Making a legacy a priority can also help to persuade powerful individuals to act morally.

"The desire to have a long-lasting impact on others is what drives people to leave a legacy"- Dr. Amit Das

According to research, when individuals think about the long term, social duty is more important to them. The theme of legacy is about reflecting on the past, embracing the present, and laying the foundation for the future. Which is preferable for planting young trees: an open field or a clearing in an old-growth forest?

"The important thing is not to stop questioning. Curiosity has its own reason for existing. One cannot help but be in awe when one contemplates the mysteries of eternity, of life, of the marvellous structure of reality. It is enough if one tries to comprehend only a little of this mystery every day."- Albert Einstein

The theory of relativity was created by the German theoretical physicist Albert Einstein who won the Nobel Prize. Additionally, the renown eccentric genius created the mass-energy equivalency equation, $E = mc2$. Although his theory of relativity is what made him most famous, his genius extended beyond that. With his Nobel Prize-winning research on the photoelectric effect, he contributed to the development of quantum mechanics and helped usher in the atomic age, despite his overall opposition to the use of nuclear weapons. He established the law of the photoelectric effect, for which he was awarded the Nobel Prize in Physics in 1921.

"It doesn't matter where you start, only where you finish. Staying true to what you believe can be the most enduring portion of your legacy."

A large portion of the study of the universe's development as well as contemporary technologies, such as lasers and computer chips, were made possible thanks to Einstein's efforts. Generations of brilliant minds will continue to be inspired by his eternal influence. His objective was to develop a "Grand Unified Theory" that would encompass all physical events, from the tiniest subatomic particles to the entire cosmos. The search for the Grand Unified Theory, however, remains one of the most actively researched areas of physics today, so Einstein's ambition did not perish with him.

"Your mind is for having ideas, not holding them."
-David Allen

His findings transformed how we view not only our planet but the entire cosmos. The cosmos as we know it was redefined by Einstein's work, which also provided us with the most understandable, elegant model to date. Black holes, the biggest cosmic monsters among them, and gravitational lensing have been discovered thanks to the theoretical physics foundation he established. He laid foundation for the development of quantum theory. It's hardly surprising that Einstein's name has come to represent scientific brilliance. The brilliance of Albert

Einstein is difficult to overstate. He was one of the most prominent physicists in the world. Generations of brilliant minds will continue to be inspired by his eternal influence.

"Our days are numbered. One of the primary goals in our lives should be to prepare for our last day. The legacy we leave is not just in our possessions, but in the quality of our lives. What preparations should we be making now? The greatest waste in all of our earth, which cannot be recycled or reclaimed, is our waste of the time that God has given us each day." — Bill Graham

Living in the now and making decisions for the present while being cognizant of an uncertain future is one of the biggest challenges facing humans. Being aware of our mortality is the dilemma's most extreme example. But we frequently face situations in life where we must make crucial judgments with little knowledge. One key aspect of the human experience is the underlying ambiguity of the future. We make an effort to live a decent, meaningful life despite the fact that we can never be certain of what is ahead for us. Nobody can live just in the now while ignoring the future. There must be a weekly rhythm and a link to a greater purpose. There must be a generational rhythm as well as a seasonal rhythm.

"You can't leave a footprint that lasts if you're always walking on tiptoe." - Marion Blakey

According to ecologists, young trees thrive when placed near more mature ones. The new tree's roots are able to follow the trails left by older trees, which allows them to establish themselves more deeply, it would appear. The new tree's roots are able to follow the trails left by older trees, which allows them to establish themselves more deeply, it would appear. The roots of many trees may really graft together over time, forming a complex, interconnected foundation under the earth. Stronger trees help weaker ones out by sharing resources in order to improve the health of the entire forest. That is legacy: a connection through time, a need for those who came before us, and a duty to those who will follow. Being human is essential to the essence of being human. Adults lose significance in their lives when, according to research, they don't feel like they are trying to leave a legacy.

"Life is not easy for any of us. But what of that? We must have perseverance and above all confidence in ourselves. We must believe that we are gifted for something and that this thing must be attained."

-Marie Curie

Marie Curie, a physicist and chemist, paved the way for women in science. She overcame obstacles and gave new concepts life. Her remarkable career is dotted with firsts, including becoming the first woman to win two Nobel Prizes, the first to have a daughter receive the prize, and many other noteworthy distinctions. Marie Curie, the first recipient of the award in two distinct categories, produced ground-breaking scientific discoveries. The groundbreaking radiation study that the Polish scientist and chemist conducted made her renowned. She conducted the initial studies into using radiation to cure tumours after discovering the two new substances, radium and polonium. But what is truly amazing is that she continued her studies during a period when she was sometimes the only female present. She stresses the value of representation and diversity in the STEM professions. We all gain when people with various identities and origins are included in science. Curie's more than 100-year-old break in the glass ceiling is even more remarkable when you consider the gender disparity that still exists today.

"We should not allow it to be believed that all scientific progress can be reduced to mechanisms, machines, gearings, even though such machinery also has its beauty. Neither do I believe that the spirit of adventure runs any risk of disappearing in our world."

- Marie Curie

Many would concur that the path toward better representation may not have been feasible without Curie's earlier attempts, even if there are still many advancements to be achieved. Without a doubt, Marie Curie was a trailblazer who paved the way for women in science. She was hailed as a "celebrity scientist" throughout her lifetime. In addition to her achievements, we should honour scientists for the boldness and determination it takes to make any kind of discovery. There are courageous workers doing their jobs right now. Although scientists have done all of those things, they are bold because undertaking something no one has ever done before entails significant emotional risks. What will you do to leave your imprint on the world now that they have all done so? Making a difference can always be done at any time.

"You cannot hope to build a better world without improving the individuals. To that end, each of us must work for his own improvement and, at the same time, share a general responsibility for all humanity, our particular duty being to aid those to whom we think we can be most useful."-Marie Curie

Most people believe that a legacy is something you leave behind or something good that happens to other people after you have lived your life. Knowing your final aim is necessary for building anything. What does leaving a living legacy mean to you? What do you hope to contribute to the world? You may be experiencing a significant societal shift or improvement that affects a sizable populace. It's also possible that your legacy will have a greater influence on a smaller group and a more personal reach. The issue of what you want your living legacy to be has no right or incorrect response. Many successful individuals I know live their legacy by giving back monetarily and by creating initiatives and materials that encourage others to be their best selves. I want to live my legacy while I'm still here because I don't want to wait until I'm gone to have the biggest influence.

"Immortality is to live your life doing good things, and leaving your mark behind." —Brandon Lee

Act now to establish your living legacy. Whatever you want your living legacy to be, start right away. Do something, however tiny. You are genuinely living your legacy today if you take any action that advances it. Your effect will be stronger the longer you can live out your legacy. There is no certainty that you will spend any time on earth. This implies that in order to have the greatest influence, you must live your legacy each and every day that you are given the gift of breathing. Any activity may be successful if you are consistent. Single deeds and legacy-making moments add up to a lasting legacy. Be certain about the steps you will take to establish your living legacy when you get up every day. Be tenacious Resistance has always been present in great attempts. This may come to you as immediate feedback from others around you or as part of the everyday rigours of a life filled with distractions.

Self-Assessment Questions:

- *You may use these questions to choose the legacy you want to leave:*

- *What values do you want to live by?*
- *How do you want your loved ones and friends to remember you?*
- *What will people remember you for outside of your immediate family and close friends?*
- *What sort of influence do you hope to have on your neighbourhood?*
- *How will your presence in the world make it a better place?*
- *What improvements do you want to make to your field?*
- *What people will you have an impact on?*
- *What knowledge would you wish to impart to the next generation?*
- *What do you wish to depart with?*

The methods listed below will help you decide what legacy you want to leave behind when you pass away. How to Leave a Legacy? Use the following concepts as a starting point to generate legacy-building ideas. Expand your understanding of the area. Through your body of work, you can leave a legacy. Here are some suggestions on how you might develop your own living legacy and ideas on how to be remembered in 100 years.

- Have a legacy driven mind simply means using your unique talents in a way that benefits society as a whole while also having personal significance for you. It's helpful to ask yourself what you are good at in order to identify what you care about. What talents do you have that may be applied to a good cause? What in the neighbourhood has significance for you? You will discover your interests and how your passions might give your life purpose by thinking about and responding to these questions.

- Do not let others' opinions affect your ability to trust yourself. The values and fundamental beliefs of people who lead meaningful lives shape their decisions and establish their short-and long-term priorities. It is what directs and moulds their daily behaviour. Although it's common to follow social conventions, there is no right or wrong way to spend your life.
- You may live your life guilt-free and be able to choose what is best for you if you trust your instincts and listen to your intuition. You must learn to trust yourself and your capacity to make the decisions that are best for you if you want to have a meaningful life.
- Motivate others one of the biggest benefits of living a life with a purpose is that you may feel proud of yourself while serving your community and learning more about your talents and abilities. If you lack this self-awareness, you cannot teach people how to help others.
- Although physical prowess is not necessary, it does call for strong feelings and convictions that may be channelled towards empowering others. You will be able to inspire others to assist others via their own personal benefits and pass it on by leading a meaningful life.
- Giving folks the confidence and freedom to pursue their lives without the constraints of surviving by appeasing someone else will inspire them to do the same for other people. Because of your words and deeds, others will feel better about themselves, which will spread positivity to others. It's a never-ending loop of good things.
- Even though life is never simple, it may be made simpler if you can learn to let go of failure and be satisfied with your goals. Your life will only get more difficult if you decide to pursue a path that isn't in line with your

purpose.

- It's crucial to go past your setbacks and find happiness in where you are right now. For instance, declining a job that contradicts your ideals or involves tasks that challenge your self-confidence doesn't make you a loser. On the contrary, it implies that your life's purpose extends beyond success and wealth. It indicates that you are fulfilled and aware of your life's mission. Power is not as significant as having inner serenity and faith in oneself.

- Additionally, you may make a scrapbook for your loved ones, a website devoted to your legacy, or record video messages for them. Give your alma mater a scholarship so that future students can benefit. If you knew you didn't have long to live, write down everything you'd want to tell your loved ones in a legacy letter. Write about your life's lessons, values, successes, and goals to really convey who you are. Consider it a sentimental heirloom. Create a blog.

- Volunteer create a nonprofit or a business from scratch. Create a memoir. Handmade objects like quilts, cedar hope boxes, or woodwork crafts should be passed on. Start a new initiative in your neighbourhood, such as a recycling campaign, a community garden, or a playground. Impart knowledge and skills. Develop your abilities, recognise your strengths, and be loyal to who you are. You may start writing a book also.

- By leaving money to your heirs, you can provide them with a solid foundation on which to build their futures. Giving money to causes close to your heart by leaving a bequest note down the family's customs and recipes.

Finally, your legacy will continue to expand and spread. There is no greater illustration of this than the numerous new versions of books that have been released after their initial release or publication when the writers' thoughts and knowledge have advanced. As you change, your legacy will as well. After a few years, I have a greater understanding and appreciation of why I set out to create this after utilising, discussing, and listening to customers' experiences, and I will continue to be open to what new insights may surface. Whatever is going on in your life, concentrating on the things you are grateful for might change your perspective.

"No matter what happens in life, be good to people. Being good to people is a wonderful legacy to leave behind."-Taylor Swift.

Making a legacy proactively is likewise non-egocentric. It is soul-driven and is simple to identify by the urge to "give back," to advance things, to share — a natural progression in service to others. My desire to create a coaching resource turned into a persistent nagging thought. Another day with a lot of possibility and opportunity is tomorrow. You should start it over completely and from scratch. Spend 10 minutes every night organising the mess and preparing your house for the next day. Your future self will appreciate it. One of the best presents we have ever received is today. Let's make good use of it and avoid throwing any away.

"The marathon of living your legacy will take you over mountainous terrain and lovely pastures. Your path's course will contribute to how you establish your living legacy. Share Your Legacy with Yourself."

The greatest way to have the most influence is to share your contribution with the entire world, even if not everyone is born with an instinctive desire to be in the spotlight. Tell everyone what your legacy is. Start with your family and friends, but watch out for those who may react negatively. Make sure you have a strong support system around you while you build your living legacy. Understanding that life is a journey rather than a destination Life is about how you get where you're going as much as where you go, despite the cliché that goes along with it. It will take you your entire life to learn how to live life to the fullest. Live your own self-authentic existence. You could be shocked by how the world reacts if you share from the heart and offer the world your gift. The Lesson we all have the capacity to make a difference when we enter this world. Why wait until after your death for your effect to be felt, whatever it may be? By taking action and allowing the world to gain from you and your contribution, you may establish your living legacy. We will experience the greatest effect when we are all carrying out our legacy!

"If you would not be forgotten as soon as you are dead, either write something worth reading or do something worth writing." —Benjamin Franklin

Mastering Your Emotions

"It is not a person or situation that affects your life; it is the meaning you give to that person or situation, which influences your emotions and actions. Your choice is to change the meaning you gave it or to change your response, in order to create the outcome you want."
-Shannon L. Alder

Understand your positive and negative emotions to leave a legacy.

We all want to know that our lives have meaning and that we have made an impact on the world. How do you define leaving a legacy? It entails leaving a mark on the future and giving back to subsequent generations. People want to feel as though their lives mattered, which is why they want to leave a legacy. You may begin acting in the manner in which you wish to be remembered. You'll be able to start doing what matters right away. You can spend your time and other resources more wisely if you know what you want your legacy to be. It will positively affect the decisions you make every day. Clarity over your desired legacy may offer your life significance and direction. You'll be able to use the legacy you're leaving to guide how you interact with others every day. You'll conduct your life as though it matters.

> *"Life has a natural rhythm; everything moves in a complex pattern, as seen in a flock of birds flying and diving together."*

Since life will take care of everything in due course, you don't need to cling to anything. Lao Tzu, a philosopher from China, is credited with saying that "Nature does not haste, but all is completed." To produce a flawless result, each condition retains its own self-organizing system. Everything functions well without any unneeded anxiety.

"If your emotional abilities aren't in hand, if you don't have self-awareness, if you are not able to manage your distressing emotions, if you can't have empathy and have effective relationships, then no matter how smart you are, you are not going to get very far."-Daniel Goleman

What is the meaning of life? One of the foundational elements of happiness is having a purpose in life. It will be more difficult to achieve lasting pleasure without a purpose, but that doesn't imply you can't be happy without one. What are some examples of a life purpose? There are several well-known goals in life, including: How to determine your own life's purpose?

> *"You can't take someone else's life's purpose and try to live it yourself while expecting to be happy. You must identify and establish your own life purpose if you wish to have a meaningful life."*

The meaning of life varies from person to person, just as happiness is something that is unique to every single person! While Elon Musk's goal in life may be to bring future concepts to life, yours may just be to give your family and kids the greatest possible existence. Many people succumb to their desires because they are guided by unconscious desires that they are unaware of.

"Positive emotions and mental states may make people more resilient to stress, like sturdy tree branches that bend but don't break when battered by a storm"
-Melanie Greenberg

We have a choice: we may accept the suffering of the world or we can make a conscious effort to think lovingly and compassionately every day. The hardest thing you have to do is learn to live with your ideas while not buying into the story they tell. Regardless of your level, money, or situation, I dare you to spend some time alone with your thoughts. They won't find their genuine selves until after that. On the one hand, we assert that we have free will, but our unconscious desires prevent us from using this freedom. Your worries and anxieties will lead you astray and should not be allowed to guide you. Be led by your creative thinking, which is where your intuitive mind resides. We can easily break the habit of paying attention to automatic ideas.

> *"Be strong enough to live the life you've always wanted, courageous enough to speak up, and brave enough to follow your heart."*

What do Oprah Winfrey, J.K. Rowling, Colonel Saunders, and Michael Jordan have in common? Despite challenging conditions, a lack of resources, other people's lack of confidence in them, maltreatment, and financial challenges, they all overcame the odds to achieve their professional ambitions. How do you know when to stop trying or cut your losses? What distinguishes perseverance from kicking a dead horse? Maybe you've got a target in your sights that you want to work toward.

> ***"The finest emotion of which we are capable is the mystic emotion." -Albert Einstein***

However, you are not getting the outcomes you were hoping for. As you consider if this is only a setback or whether you should press forward in faith, uncertainty sets in that perhaps you are going about things the incorrect way. The choice to endure is one of the hardest ones to make, whether you decide to keep fishing in a certain area on the lake or stay in a bad marriage in the hopes that things will improve. When a change in strategy or direction is necessary, only you can decide. Only you can decide whether it is appropriate to put time and effort into a failed relationship or career endeavour. The trick is to change your behaviour rather than give up. As long as you keep trying, you will succeed.

> *"Everyone who wants to find a perfect companion may, with the exception of the one who gives up."*

Consider the following ideas to keep going when you're feeling discouraged and unsure when you've worked hard for success but only see evidence of the opposite. Don't you ever have the sense that your life is passing you by without you doing anything to enjoy it?

> ***Do you realise that you have already lived over half of your remaining life?***

- Live your life on your terms and spend less time trying to swim against the current.
- Follow the flow of life and keep an open mind.
- Realise that there are no mistakes as you take one stride forward and two steps back.

Your greatest gift comes from taking that one step back because it gives you the information and expertise you need to achieve your objective. Follow your passion, but don't be too set in your ways about how you'll get there. Accept what seems to be a dead end as a blessing in disguise rather than fight it. Allow life to throw open doors and illuminate previously unimagined paths to your goals. Giving up is not surrendering. It is a step in the procedure. It is an accepting state. Without the capacity to allow, you will not be able to persist.

> *"Success has several facets, including not only material wealth but also good physical, mental, and emotional health."*

We require the ability to express ourselves freely as well as the ability to love and feel valued. Success in one area does not support the other. This explains why some individuals appear to have it all yet aren't actually content. We are all born with immense potential. We all have untapped potential that is just waiting to be fulfilled. We all have this emotion inside of us. The sadness is that by ignoring the manifestation of this creativity, we are doing the gravest imaginable offence. Unfortunately, these special abilities and skills become a poisonous, deadly force when they go undeveloped.

"Only if you invest your emotions in what matters to you, will life become powerful and really meaningful."
- Sadguru

We develop harmful behaviours as a result of this act of suppression, the main one of which is self-sabotage. We have been instructed to hold back our might and to cease believing in our natural instincts and fundamental wisdom. The weight placed upon us and its resultant impact on the amount of time we have to enjoy life keeps us helpless. Encourage joyful emotions finding meaning can be aided by cultivating good feelings like appreciation. Because caring for others, discovering your purpose in life, and general well-being are all correlated with happy feelings. You may be better able to concentrate on how you can make a difference in the world if you have a direct connection to your happy feelings.

"No matter how many people you encounter in your life, all that matters is finding the genuine ones who will love you for who you are and guide you toward becoming the person you should be."

Developing an attitude of thankfulness enables you to take stock of your benefits and spread them to others. This is frequently regarded as a case when someone may find "found" money. They give their newly discovered money to others as part of their blessing. A life lived with purpose and thankfulness might be characterised as being grateful for the ability to connect with things in life that aren't quantifiable and to distinguish between desires and necessities. The common positive emotions are love, serenity, forgiveness, awe, joy, interest, hope, pride, amusement, and inspiration.

"We become more receptive to the beneficial impacts that good emotions have on our resilience and overall well-being when we include more love, kindness, empathy, and compassion into our lives."

Positive feelings are highly regarded and actively sought after. Positive feelings, however, may have long-term advantages in significant areas, such as jobs, physical health, and interpersonal relationships, beyond simply being enjoyable. The focus of research so far has been on the more general purposes of happy emotions. The broaden-and-build hypothesis holds that people may develop their social, psychological, and intellectual capabilities by expanding their thought-action repertoires in response to pleasant feelings.

"The best and most beautiful things in the world cannot be seen or even touched. They must be felt with the heart."
– Helen Keller

According to recent research, people may be motivated to participate in constructive activities that will better themselves by experiencing happy feelings, especially thankfulness. We suggest and provide evidence for the idea that being grateful motivates people to make an attempt to better themselves through increasing connectivity, elevation, humility, and some negative feelings like indebtedness. Social media represents the carefully curated lifestyles we want the world to see. Due to the fact that social media is now carefully curated to reflect the lifestyles we want others to see us leading, it often provides an inaccurate reflection of how individuals actually live. As we anxiously compare our social media clout based on the number of followers we have, there is pressure to provide the most "likeable" material. We now have a superpower thanks to social media, but we might not have been utilising it properly.

"Emotion is more powerful than reason. Emotion is the driving force behind thinking and reasoning. Emotional intelligence increases the mind's ability to make positive, brilliant decisions." – Dr. T.P. Chia

Thanks to the digital world, we can communicate with almost everyone on the planet in real time. It enables us to stay in touch with far-off relatives and friends. It enables us to openly share our ideas with the world so that they might be seen and perhaps benefited from. But we frequently use it for slander, harassment, and trolling. It serves as a place for us to express our emotional suffering. We use it to quarrel and fight with people over unimportant issues.

"The only thing that stands between you and your wellbeing is a simple fact: you have allowed your thoughts and emotions to take instruction from the outside rather than within."- Sadguru

So now consider this: What if every word, social media post, email, and uploaded image were to remain there indefinitely? A digital trail that determines how others will remember you? In your current form, would you still utilise social media? Most likely not. Would your opinion change if there was no visible display of likes and followers? Does our lust for social currency alter who we are at our core? You might not think that being emotionally aware has much to do with business.

"Don't shut down your emotions. Embrace them. Your emotions are your internal compass telling you whether or not you are on track. Use them to help cultivate your passions or motivate you to change situations and circumstances that hold you back from achieving your goals." – Jillian Michaels

Nevertheless, several studies have indicated that unfavourable work environments might affect the well-being of families that have employees as members. In other words, employees bring the stress and hostility they experience at work into their personal lives and relationships. According to a recent Harvard Business Review article, the effect was that the stress people face at work crosses over to and hinders the functioning and well-being of family members, including harming children's academic achievement.

"We can never obtain peace in the outer world until we make peace with ourselves." — Dalai Lama

Negative emotion storage is detrimental to your health. It will ultimately find a way out, and a sympathetic ear is the best place for it. Keeping difficulties to oneself can result in a variety of physical and mental stress, including headaches, stomach cramps, and restlessness, without you even realising it. Speak to someone, whether a friend or a professional, if you're feeling overwhelmed and in need of assistance. They could provide you with the suggestions or guidance you need.

Are you leading the best life you can? You are not living life to the fullest if you answered "no," "I'm not sure," or "maybe" to the question above. This truly shouldn't be the case considering that you are in charge of creating your own life experience. Everyone has good and bad days, but the most important thing is to make the most of each day, regardless of how it goes. Be prepared to fail.

"The more mistakes you make and the more experience you have, the higher your chances of success."

You may occasionally feel anxious, concerned, in pain, or utterly bored and try to hide this truth. Take control of your emotions by noticing when you experience odd highs or lows and considering why. List the events from the previous week that gave you energy and made you feel down on paper. You may create such a list each week and take one step away from "depressors" and toward "energizers." This will gradually liberate your potential. However, there are numerous personality tests that are available that may help you identify your inherent traits and talents. Observing your feelings is a terrific way to appreciate your individuality and potential. Attempt the Strengthsfinder, Myers-Briggs, Enneagram, or other assessment.

"Ordinary people think merely of spending time, great people think of using it." -Arthur Schopenhauer

Take careful note of the lessons you may use from each incident if you want to get better. Be ready to be let down. Many people go to great lengths to avoid being let down. They learn to negatively connect with disappointment. However, disappointment is a normal aspect of being human since it reveals your actual emotions. Instead of resisting it, accept it. Learn to control your emotions and unhappiness to achieve more in life. I believe that living is a beautiful experience.

"Thoughts and emotions come from the same source. Thoughts are the dry expressions of the mind, emotions are juicy. The way you think is the way you feel."- Sadguru

Handling Your Rejection

"Go beyond the limitations we unconsciously create for ourselves, and live our life to the fullest. If you shift from unwillingness to willingness, from inertia to effervescence, your life will become joyful; your journey will become effortless."- Sadguru

You must move from rejection to transformation to leave a legacy.

When we get into the idea that "I think, therefore I am," we become unable to separate ourselves from our ideas. Your thoughts are not all that you are. They are not the reason you suffer or are unhappy; instead, you suffer because you connect with them and get attached to them. When we think that our thoughts are reality, chaos results.

"No one cares how much you know, until they know how much you care." -Theodore Roosevelt

People act out their thoughts in troubled parts of the world, which causes issues. We don't need to participate in peace marches or protests to achieve peace; it is much easier than that. It starts with our ideas and spreads across our lives and those of others. The matter is how justifiable our cause, when we hold onto our ideas with hostility, violence, and suffering spread over the globe. Peace is fostered through practising non-aggression. Think about an unkind thought you could have about someone else. If it is given too much attention, it agitates other ideas and produces undesirable results.

"When dealing with people, remember you are not dealing with creatures of logic, but with creatures of emotion." -Dale Carnegie

Steve Jobs is credited for helping Apple grow into the world's largest corporation. However, it is really astonishing to learn that the multi-billion dollars firm, which currently employs over 130 thousand people, was first founded by just two people in a garage. Additionally, it should be noted that this outstanding entrepreneur was sacked and let go from the business where he first began his career. In addition, after discovering his potential and talents, Steve Jobs moved forward with the creation of the largest firm in the world, known as "Apple."

"It's not that I'm so smart, it's just that I stay with problems longer."-Albert Einstein

It was considerably more crucial for Bill Gates to learn from failure than it was to rejoice in victory. This brilliant businessman, a Harvard dropout, is responsible for making Microsoft the largest software corporation. In addition, he was well-known for the greatest business failure in history, Traf-O-Data, a self-owned company entity. Bill Gates' whole investment was lost, and regrettably, even the education could not be finished. But his intense drive and enthusiasm for everything related to computer programming inspired him to start the world's largest software firm under the trade name "Microsoft."

"Many of life's failures are people who did not realize how close they were to success when they gave up."-Thomas Edison

The inventor of the delicious milk-chocolate delight we all adore, Milton Hershey, wasn't immediately successful. He had previously worked at a nearby candy manufacturer before starting his own candy company. But when he made the decision to go out on his own, he utterly failed. Despite suffering two more setbacks, he went back to the family farm and mastered the technique of producing beautiful milk chocolate candies, which we now enjoy in the form of Hershey's chocolate.

"Failure is only the opportunity to begin again, this time more intelligently."-Henry Ford

Walt Disney's first job was getting sacked by a newspaper because he wasn't innovative enough. Later, since they were thought to be "too disturbing for women," his Mickey Mouse cartoons were rejected. The fact that "The Three Little Pigs" only had four characters added insult to injury. The majority of the time, we tend to blame fate for our failure.

> *"The number of rejections you experience is typically inversely correlated with your level of success."*

The enemies of success are rejection and anxiety. If you postpone making difficult calls out of concern that others may reject you (such as clients, workers, coworkers, or colleagues), your effectiveness will suffer. But overcoming that fear is just the beginning. If you truly want to succeed, you must figure out how to use rejection as a tool to propel you closer to your long-term objectives.

"We all learn lessons in life. Some stick, some don't. I have always learned more from rejection and failure than from acceptance and success." – Henry Rollins

Imagine you get the opportunity to present your elevator pitch to a significant investor. Despite your best efforts, the investor just tells you to "go away" or, worse yet, "your concept stinks; we'll contact you." If you were hoping to get any investment capital, it is undoubtedly a dismal result. But why would you feel "rejected" as opposed to, say, annoyed, irate, or sad? The reason is that, rather than focusing on the problem itself, you took the investor's remarks personally and allowed them to make you feel horrible about yourself.

"You only have to do a very few things right in your life so long as you don't do too many things wrong." --Warren Buffett

If you feel like you are receiving too many rejections, examine the expectations of other individuals who are doing what you are. Salespeople, for example, may make 100 calls before identifying a prospect; similarly, entrepreneurs may give presentations to dozens of investors before receiving financing. If you are emotionally invested in the other person, disassociate yourself from the result of the scenario. Even if the prospect you've been courting for months doesn't end up buying, you've still created a wonderful business connection.

"I hated every minute of training, but I said, 'Don't quit. Suffer now and live the rest of your life as a champion." – Muhammad Ali

If you believe the other person to be extremely significant, balance your appreciation with a healthy dose of realism. Even well-known business moguls are often below-average performers who luck into success. Even if not, they are still just regular individuals like you and me and not gods on earth. After gaining some perspective on your feelings, it's important to use some practical reasoning to distinguish between legitimate and unjustified complaints.

"I take rejection as someone blowing a bugle in my ear to wake me up and get going, rather than retreat." – Sylvester Stallone

When a person refuses to do what you ask them to because of anything within your control, this is a justified refusal. When your "failure" occurred as a result of an arbitrary event outside of your control, that rejection is illegitimate. Consider the scenario when you meet with a client and say something foolish, like the wrong client's name. The customer's departure is a legitimate rejection because you were to blame for the triggering event. Success isn't always more than a numbers game.

"Your work is going to fill a large part of your life, and the only way to be truly satisfied is to do what you believe is great work. And the only way to do great work is to love what you do. If you haven't found it yet, keep looking. Don't settle. As with all matters of the heart, you'll know when you find it." – Steve Jobs

I sent the concept for my first business book to a lot of editors and received a lot of "rejection letters." Instead of giving up, I began each day by spreading the letters out on the ground and using them as stepping stones. A lot of individuals are stopped in their tracks by the pain of rejection. In an effort to reduce the possibility of more rejections, they started acting cautiously. But psychologically powerful individuals don't behave that way.

Whether they were rejected by a potential love partner or passed over for a promotion, they bounce back stronger than before.

"It is during our darkest moments that we must focus to see the light." – Aristotle

You could feel better for a moment by putting on a brave front and saying things like, "I didn't want that job anyhow." However, attempting to make yourself—or people around you—believe that you don't care won't help you in the long run to mend your injured ego. When someone is mentally strong, they will disclose when they are truly ashamed, wounded, or dissatisfied. By confronting their feelings, they can recover from their suffering in a healthy way.

"If you aren't getting rejected on a daily basis, your goals aren't ambitious enough."— Chris Dixon

It might be easy to exaggerate your bad luck or make dire predictions about how a single rejection would cause you to live in sorrow for the rest of your life. You'll remain trapped if you think statements like "I'll never move up the corporate ladder" or "No one will ever believe in me." People with strong minds won't have a sad party. Instead, they tell themselves that being rejected isn't the end of the world and they create a strategy for moving on. You probably aren't trying to reach your full potential if you aren't getting rejected.

"Rejection is evidence that you stretched yourself and sought to widen your horizons. People with strong mental faculties are proud of themselves for being ready to push themselves. They understand that being declined or passed over demonstrates

that they are truly enjoying life to the fullest."

If an employer rejects your application, you could assume that you are totally unqualified. Or, you can conclude you're ugly if a partner rejects you. However, making broad generalisations based on one person's viewpoint will only make you slower. People with good mental faculties don't let other people's opinions determine their sense of value. Instead, despite being rejected, they are aware of who they are and what they are capable of. It might be tempting to listen to your inner critic when you're feeling bad. But telling yourself you're a failure or that you'll never be successful will simply make rejection hurt worse.

> "*Rejection is a hard emotion to deal with and an even harder message to hear. When we are faced with rejection, it can be a hit to our ego, or it can make us question if we are good enough.*"

People with high mental faculties are kind to themselves. They don't criticise themselves for their shortcomings and speak to themselves like a valued friend might. They heal more quickly and efficiently thanks to their positive self-talk. If you're willing to learn, rejection may be a useful instructor. You won't become better by criticising yourself, coming up with reasons why you failed, or placing blame on others.

> "*Sometimes what we learn from rejection, ends up ultimately making us the best version of ourselves, and in the best possible position.*"

People with high mental faculties not only put up with discomfort, but also use it as a teaching opportunity. They constantly reflect on what they have learned. They get more aware and more determined with each rejection they receive. If you're not careful, rejection may halt you in your tracks. However, assuming you're "out of your league" will restrict your possibilities. Mentally tough individuals allow themselves time to heal after a particularly traumatic rejection. They search for other possibilities once they're prepared.

"Life is 10% what happens to you and 90% how you react to it."- Charles R. Swindoll

Success constantly puts itself forward rather than the made-up myths and looks past the ridiculous justifications. Success is the outcome of strong perseverance and attention when going forward along the working road.

"A failure is not always a mistake. It may simply be the best one can do under the circumstances. The real mistake is to stop trying." -B.F. Skinner

CHAPTER FOUR

Design Your Destiny

"It's not whether the glass is half empty or half full, it's who is pouring the water. The key in business and success at any endeavor is doing your best to control your destiny. You can't always do it, but you have to take every opportunity you can to be as prepared as-and ahead of-the competition as you possibly can be."

-Mark Cuban

You can leave a legacy because you control your destiny.

You are in charge of your own destiny. You have undoubtedly heard this a lot in your life. Maybe this resonates with you, or maybe you feel that the sentiment condescendingly oversimplifies the difficulties of life that might restrict your alternatives. Whether or not you feel like you have complete control over your destiny, the truth is that you do. Controlling your ideas is a key component in shaping (or influencing) your future. The viewpoint that you have influence over what happens rather than feeling as though something is happening to you is created by viewing problems as opportunities. Because of this, you may take action and affect change as opposed to just accepting your circumstances.

"Experience is not what happens to you--it's how you interpret what happens to you." -Aldous Huxley

You ought to take into account how you view yourself. Remind yourself that you are never a passive victim of your circumstances since pride is something to exercise. You have the power to control your circumstances and alter your course.

"Control your own destiny or someone else will."-Jack Welch

A life with meaning is abundant when you operate from the level of the soul. Please bear with me as we go a little deeper into this. Living from the soul level entails letting go of our ideas about how life ought to be. You have a more profound understanding of your spiritual existence. It necessitates focusing on your actual essence, independent of your worldview. These are ideas you developed to help you make sense of your surroundings, but they serve no more purpose than a motorcycle's training wheels.

"You are the master of your destiny. You can influence, direct and control your own environment. You can make your life what you want it to be."-Napoleon Hill

When things do not go as planned or as we had hoped, we frequently blame it on fate. The opposite is also true in that some individuals frequently blame others' success on their fate rather than recognising the effort they put into their accomplishments. In other words, we associate our choices with our future.

We frequently believe that destiny, a great power, governs our lives rather than ourselves. What one should understand, though, is that a man's fate is determined by his mind and the thoughts he puts into action. Thank goodness Walt decided to ignore all of his detractors and pursue his ambitions instead of listening to them, as a result of which we now have the Disney corporation. A determined intellect might lead you to destinations you never imagined. That is why the phrase "It's all in the head" is so popular. Only the choices we make will determine our future.

"All success in life, whether material or spiritual, starts with the thoughts that you put into your mind every second of every minute of every day. Your outer world reflects the state of your inner world. By controlling the thoughts that you think and the way you respond to the events of your life, you begin to control your destiny."-Rohit Sharma

Successful individuals handle situations differently. They just alter their reactions to the occurrences until they get the desired results. You have the power to alter your behaviour, communication style, mental representations of the world, and way of thinking (the things you do). You essentially just have control over it. Unfortunately, the majority of us are controlled by our routines. We become mired in conditioned reactions to our partners and kids, our coworkers, our clients and customers, our students, and the rest of the world.

"Your destiny is to fulfill those things upon which you focus most intently. So choose to keep your focus on that which is truly magnificent, beautiful, uplifting and joyful. Your life is always moving toward something."-Ralph Marston

You must learn to regulate your ideas, pictures, dreams, daydreams, and actions. Your thoughts, words, and actions must all be deliberate and in line with your mission, beliefs, and objectives. Sometimes you come up with a brilliant concept right away that you can develop and run with.

Everything seems to be going great until you have a setback. You get punched in the gut by failure, leaving you with aching wounds and no choice but to whine about what might have been. Change your replies if you don't like the results.

"The law of harvest is to reap more than you sow. Sow an act, and you reap a habit. Sow a habit and you reap a character. Sow a character and you reap a destiny."- James Allen

Our ideas are the embodiment of our minds, and our actions are the result of those thoughts. One just cannot sit back, fold his arms, and claim that everything in his or her life is the result of fate. Our way of thinking and the way we see the world directly affect how we live. Only the choices we make will determine our future. For instance, if a person has a strong will and a determined attitude, the decision-making process and how the choice is carried out will eventually establish that person's fate, which will finally determine their destiny.

"Life is not always going to be roses and rainbows. You are going to have uncomfortable moments. It's what we do with those moments that is going to count and determine our destiny."-Lana

We are solely responsible for our own destinies. Whether things turn out better or worse depends entirely on how we perceive and respond to the events that occur in our lives. One's fate is decided by the way they think and behave. Our thoughts have a major role in how we behave, and our actions play a major role in how we are seen by others. Therefore, a man with control over his thoughts has power over his actions, which in turn gives him control over any circumstances in life that may eventually determine his fate.

"Your destiny is to fulfill those things upon which you focus most intently. So choose to keep your focus on that which is truly magnificent, beautiful, uplifting and joyful. Your life is always moving toward something."-Ralph Marston

Considering that everything is temporary, try to avoid being attached to people, places, or events. Dread is the source of clinging, which breeds more fear. Change your thoughts to more powerful ones so that you can easily allow what is required to flow into your experience. Don't hold onto things you don't need anymore. Consider repurposing it if you haven't used it in the past three months. Less tangible possessions free us from having to handle more. I'm not advocating leading a simple existence; rather, you shouldn't look to worldly items to bolster your sense of identity.

"The high destiny of the individual is to serve rather than to rule."-Albert Einstein

Michael Joseph Jackson, better known as the "King of Pop," was a multi-talented musical performer who had great success both as a solo artist, best-selling American singer, songwriter, and dancer. MJ began his musical career at the young age of 5 with encouragement from his father, Joseph Walter Jackson, and went on to become acknowledged as the greatest entertainer of the 20th century. He was in the spotlight for more than four decades thanks to his well-known moonwalk dancing style and fashion specialties like his crystal gloves and the 1980s trophy jacket trend that was immortalised. The second best-selling album in history, Thriller, included Jackson's most well-known work. He then went on to create a string of successful singles, including Bad, Dangerous, Off the Wall, History, and Invincible. Among his greatest accomplishments are 31

Guinness World Records, 13 Grammy Awards, 26 American Music Awards, five consecutive Billboard Top 10 singles, etc.

"Anything that happens in your life was meant to happen. It is your destiny. I was destined to have the life I have now, and I can't have any regrets."- Zlatan Ibrahimovic

Whatever you choose to call it—destiny, fate, karma, serendipity—the notion that life is predetermined by forces outside of our control is an age-old one. It exists in every culture on earth, including ancient Chinese narrative and Greek mythology. But what if fate wasn't actually real? What if you had influence over your future? You have acknowledged your internal centre of control if you think you are in charge of your own destiny. It means that you accept responsibility for your thoughts, actions, and results. This method of thinking can help you become unstoppable. You may learn to take charge of your future. You must first embrace who you are and where you are right now in order to take control of your future. You'll run out of things to do if you trick yourself into thinking that you're further along in your goals than you actually are.

"Your life will be no better than the plans you make and the action you take. You are the architect and builder of your own life, fortune, destiny."- Alfred A. Montapert

Don't delude yourself into thinking your life is worse than it is, though. Take a step back and consider your situation differently. Increase your awareness of yourself and embrace the truth. If you don't know where you're starting from, you can't develop a strategy to control your fate. Accepting reality does not entail passively accepting your fate without taking any action. It entails taking responsibility for the things you can alter and letting go of the things you can't. You have no influence over what people believe or do. You have no power over the market. Your own mentality is the only thing you have control over. To do that, you must challenge the self-talk you believe in and replace it with an empowering one.

"The torment of precautions often exceeds the dangers to be avoided. It is sometimes better to abandon one's self to destiny."- Napoleon Bonaparte

Because of the level of brilliance he showed in his work, he is regarded as one of the greatest individuals in the world, and others enrol in music production classes in an effort to emulate him. All of us who live in this beautiful world aspire to success. We all have the innate drive to succeed and move steadily in the direction of greater success, regardless of whether the person in question is a kid, a young adult, or an elderly person. Any location, including schools, universities, coaching, professional settings such as companies, workplaces, etc., to name a few, may usually exhibit a competitive mindset.

"We need a spirit of victory, a spirit that will carry us to our rightful place under the sun, a spirit which can recognize that we, as inheritors of a proud civilization, are entitled to our rightful place on this planet. If that indomitable spirit were to arise, nothing can hold us from achieving our rightful destiny."- C. V. Raman

When compared to the effort we put into achieving success, we frequently have higher expectations and hope that it will arrive sooner rather than later. If it does not, we tend to become upset and eventually sink farther into the pit of inferiority. The majority of individuals have observed this circumstance, when regular and committed efforts are neglected and only failures are celebrated. Such instances may be found anywhere in the world. The majority of famous people have had significant setbacks in their battles with life. Nevertheless, they persisted in their paths to success and eventually experienced enormous success in their specialised industries. They never let their race, religion, or any other distinction stand in the way of their achievement.

"Choosing your new way of life when do we truly stop and realise that our behaviours are harming us? How do you go about developing healthy habits and a new way of life?"

On the basis of events and observations from previous lives, one's conception of man may alter. Your thoughts will get better as you watch and learn more, which will improve how you think and behave. Successful individuals spend a lot of time considering what and how they should act, and it is this way of thinking that has enabled them to change their fate and achieve better things in life. A strong and capable intellect is capable of great things. A man's ability to regulate his thoughts and use willpower is what enables him to achieve so much in life. The mindset that "it was destined to be" brings about disaster because it causes us to give up on our efforts to continuously work toward success and instead to use this as a justification for our failures.

"Every individual soul chooses the significant people in that life. Destiny will place you in the particular circumstance; it will dictate that you will encounter a particular person, at a certain time, place."- Brian Weiss

Therefore, we should alter our perspectives and behaviour and continue to make attempts and endeavour in the quest for our achievement, which will define our fate. We can absolutely change our fate if we can change our minds. In our hands, it is. Just three years before the release of the first Harry Potter novel, Harry Potter and The Philosopher's Stone, in 1994, J.K. Rowling had recently gone through a divorce, was receiving government assistance, and could barely afford to feed her infant. She had to physically type each version to send to publishers since she could not afford a computer or even the expense of photocopying the 90,000-word novel at the time she was shopping it around. It was repeatedly turned down until a tiny London publisher named Bloomsbury decided to resubmit it after the CEO's eight-year-old daughter fell in love with it.

"As long as we are persistence in our pursuit of our deepest destiny, we will continue to grow. We cannot choose the day or time when we will fully bloom. It happens in its own time."-Denis Waitley

As you overcome challenges and correct errors, you will amass evidence that you are a strong woman, evidence that you can draw on when you begin to doubt your abilities. You always have a choice in how you react to the things that life throws your way, whether they are good or negative. You can choose to run away from a difficulty, let it overtake you, or make an effort to conquer it. Although none of these choices will always be the ideal ones for you in the long term, strive to be aware of your possibilities.

Occasionally, despite your greatest efforts, you will fall short. You could fail at social contact, be unable to rescue a dying relationship, or fail to accomplish a goal. These things have the power to make you feel bad about yourself and set you back considerably. When anything goes wrong, take a time to gather your thoughts before deciding whether to try again. Perhaps you can mend the bond or begin a new one with someone else. You can apologise for making a social faux pas and elaborate on your intentions.

"I believe that you control your destiny, that you can be what you want to be. You can also stop and say, 'No, I won't do it, I won't behave this way anymore. I'm lonely and I need people around me, maybe I have to change my methods of behaving,' and then you do it."-Leo Buscaglia

Sometimes, falling short of your goals might even be beneficial. Being knocked down may ignite a fire within you that motivates you to succeed. You can always learn from your failures, so take the time to reflect on what went wrong in your last attempt and make plans on how to improve going forward. You will learn new things about yourself, the best ways for you to work, and the greatest strategies to get things done. Other times, failure may help you gain perspective and see that what you were doing wasn't feasible or appropriate for you. There are numerous ways forward; pick one that appeals to you and makes you optimistic about the future.

"You can't connect the dots looking forward; you can only connect them looking backward. So you have to trust that the dots will somehow connect in your future. You have to trust in something – your gut, destiny, life, karma, whatever. This approach has never let me down, and it has made all the difference in my life. "-Steve Jobs

You will increase your personal confidence while boosting other people's confidence in you. They will be impressed by your grace when they see how you face problems head-on and get through barriers in life. When others respect you, you will be exposed to more possibilities and have the freedom to select which ones you want to pursue. All of a sudden, you're back in charge! Keep in mind the things you can manage when life seems out of control and you lack agency. A shift in perspective might set off a chain of events that will transform you into the master of your own destiny.

"If you believe in destiny, then you know that you have a purpose. You know things happen for a reason, and that you should find out how to live up to that essence of what you're supposed to do and which direction you are determined to take."- V. Noot

Many people make unwise judgments in the haste of life and abuse alcohol or drugs. Many other people struggle with sadness or anxiety. We experience a crisis—a collapse on the physical, emotional, or spiritual levels—when life goes on uncontrolled. Recovery depends on both physical and mental wellbeing. Creating healthy behaviours and drawing on spiritual inspiration. The incredible power of inspiration examines the tale of our lives first from the outside in, starting with our circumstances and ending with our feelings, and then from the inside out, starting with our dreams and ending with the outer world. This ground-breaking holistic approach to the body, mind, and spirit enables readers to break bad habits and create healthier, more fulfilling lives.

"Destiny is a name often given in retrospect to choices that had dramatic consequences."- J.K. Rowling

Limiting beliefs, or the unfavourable things we tell ourselves about who we are and how the world operates, only prevent you from having complete control over your future. The motivation behind your actions, or your driving force, may also be gleaned from your connections. Six human needs—certainty, importance, diversity, love/connection, development, and contribution—are what motivate each of us. We all require these things on some level, but each of us has a primary need that dominates all others.

"No one saves us but ourselves. No one can and no one may. We ourselves must walk the path."
— *Gautama Buddha*

You'll be able to better manage your destiny if you see your life in this light, since you'll be able to identify and meet your needs in healthy ways. Although it is a survival mechanism, fear doesn't always help us, just like in relationships. Living in fear prevents you from ever learning how to master your destiny. You must learn to control your fear rather than allow it to control you if you want to reach your full potential and become the best version of yourself. Be open and honest with your spouse. Take action to launch the company you've always wanted. Enroll in a public speaking course. Do whatever it is you're terrified of right now.

> *"Most of us believe in destiny and fate; it is with that belief we are able to live our lives with confidence and be hopeful about the times to come."*

This book is an enlightening voyage through one's own life, including our past, present, and future. We will re-vision and re-cast our life's tale as explorers in our own lives by discovering our deepest inspiration, our happiest emotions, and expressing our ambitions. The author tells readers how to gracefully navigate the difficulties of life while remaining energised and thoroughly grounded. We may effectively realise our full potential, change the narrative, and adopt a new way of life. With the help of this potent technique, readers may become their own heroes, rewrite their own stories, and empower themselves to lead fulfilling lives.

"You are the creator of your destiny." -Swami Vivekanand

CHAPTER FIVE

Finding Purpose In Life

"The purpose of life is not to be happy. It is to be useful, to be honourable, to be compassionate, to have it make some difference that you have lived and lived well." — Ralph Waldo Emerson

Find your purpose and unlock your best life.

The word "purpose" is frequently misused. I've observed a lot of individuals searching for a higher meaning in life, such as a type of world-saving mission. Basically, they were looking for something to satisfy their egos and make them feel really exceptional. The concept of "purpose" is distinct. You don't have to make the world better. It's simply a matter of changing your focus from "what you can take from life today" to "how you can contribute to life today." That's my list, then.

"Our prime purpose in this life is to help others. And if you can't help them, at least don't hurt them."- Dalai Lama

What do we define as the purpose of our lives? Purpose must begin with each of us as an individual. What is the mission we see for ourselves? Let's start by discussing purpose in terms of human psychology. While some could contend that each of us has a distinct mission, the bulk of us have two characteristics and will identify with them. Development is the first. Being the best version of ourselves is our top priority as humans, along with actualizing our potential and growing to our fullest potential.

"I truly believe that everything that we do and everyone that we meet is put in our path for a purpose. There are no accidents; we're all teachers - if we're willing to pay attention to the lessons we learn, trust our positive instincts and not be afraid to take risks or wait for some miracle to come knocking at our door."

-Marla Gibbs

Millions of species, 30,000 distinct varieties of life, and over 7 billion people all cohabit and provide for one another on Earth in their own unique ways. It's incredible how much is out there that we don't know and that has to be discovered. As long as you are in this world, keep embracing life. Only in this way can we continue to exist. Consider others. Giving back to the community is a wonderful way to give life purpose again, which might frequently feel like it's going downhill otherwise. There are countless ways to help others, such as maintaining an elderly neighbor's garden or volunteering at a local charity shop. Yes, you are performing this labour gratuitously and for complete strangers, but someone's day will suddenly be made better because of your kindness. Giving back is the most fulfilling thing you can do.

"True happiness... is not attained through self-gratification, but through fidelity to a worthy purpose."- Helen Keller

People who are only interested in making money for themselves will typically find that their pursuit of pleasure or collecting material possessions delivers a declining sense of fulfilment, and life will become meaningless and dull. Our ambition to develop our purpose must be grounded in a genuine desire to act morally. We will be met with cynicism and scepticism if our activities are seen as just another effort to persuade our staff to be more productive or profitable.

"The purpose of human life is to serve, and to show compassion and the will to help others."- Albert Schweitzer

The notion that everything happens in life for a reason lies at the very core of a life lived with purpose. The purpose of adversity is to teach us the lessons we need to know in order to advance. When something doesn't work out the way we expected it to, it's because we weren't ready for the new chance that came along. When we keep our attention solely on the present, we only have an impact on the aspects of the world that we have the power to alter. Do not let dogma, which is living according to the conclusions of other people's thinking, capture you. Keep your inner voice from being drowned out by the clamour of other people's thoughts. The most essential thing to remember is to have the guts to listen to your heart and intuition because they somehow already know who you are meant to be. "Everything else is just a side note." Apple Inc.

- *Right now, how do you feel about your life?*
- *Do you experience daily elation?*
- *Do you look forward to the next event with anticipation?*

Purposeful describes the steps to help you live a full life—a life of purpose, direction, and meaning—whatever that is for you. It includes action guides and activities. It's about becoming the kind of person you want to be and living the kind of life you want to live. If they don't have a plan for their time on earth, they will never be prolific and a blessing to their family, society, nation, and generations. The majority of individuals have a routine existence that involves getting up in the morning, going after money, returning home, eating, drinking, and engaging in sexual activity, and repeating the cycle until death arrives and takes man away.

"Everyone has a purpose in life and a unique talent to give to others. And when we blend this unique talent with service to others, we experience the ecstasy and exultation of own spirit, which is the ultimate goal of all goals."
-Kallam Anji Reddy

Our eagerness to trust life outweighs our capacity for reason as long as we maintain this awareness. So, effortless living is the readiness to let go of our urge for desired results and accept the flow experience. We release situations that no longer benefit us rather than frantically grasping at life. To let go means to mentally and emotionally distance oneself from circumstances that are out of our control. Instead of moving with the flow, energy is wasted fighting against life. The egoic mind asserts that it is far more intelligent than that which directs the stars and planets. Given that we are a minor component in a carefully planned process, we are aware of the fallacy of that assumption.

"When you're surrounded by people who share a passionate commitment around a common purpose, anything is possible."- Howard Schultz

The Almighty never acts haphazardly; he gave everything, including people, a reason when he created it. According to the Bhagvad Gita, the Almighty created man and assigned him to live on this earth for the primary purpose of creation. The Man was to rule over the earth by procreating, multiplying, and replenishing it.

Before giving birth to man, almighty, a loving and principled father, created everything that man would need to enjoy life. However, he also established rules by which men must carry out their responsibilities as rulers. Finding one's life's purpose has, for many people, become an illusion. Yet there are guidelines for leading a meaningful life that, when followed, will lead to people bearing fruit and becoming blessings. Although unwanted pregnancies are possible, no one's existence on earth is intended to be in vain. Every person on earth has a purpose that almighty has for them; a purpose that, even if they are unaware of it, requires them to produce fruit and be of benefit.

"Your work is going to fill a large part of your life, and the only way to be truly satisfied is to do what you believe is great work. And the only way to do great work is to love what you do. If you haven't found it yet, keep looking. Don't settle. As with all matters of the heart, you'll know when you find it." — Steve Jobs

The desire for a feeling of purpose has long been acknowledged as a fundamental human need and a significant source of motivation in life. It is said that purpose is to the soul what air is to our lungs. We find hope and optimism in purpose. It encourages a favourable attitude and an innate drive for whatever we are doing or seeking. What purpose is to our soul, breath is to our lungs. When a person has a clear sense of goal and that objective is engrained in his or her culture, it has a profoundly transformative effect on an individual. It boosts people's productivity and promotes appropriate behaviour that serves that goal. Additionally, it helps the business connect emotionally with its clientele. Let's examine each one separately.

"The purpose of life is undoubtedly to know oneself. We can't do it unless we learn to identify with everything that lives. The instrument of this knowledge is boundless, selfless service."
- Mahatma Gandhi

When you discover how to live a more purposeful life, you stop waiting for better circumstances and start appreciating the present. Instead of basing your happiness on something that may or may not happen in the future, enjoy what is happening around you right now. Keep in mind that you should be glad because you were a part of the beginning of something new rather than unhappy because something has ended.

Our sorrows are caused by our sinful reactions. Mohandas Karamchand Gandhi, usually referred to as "Mahatma" or the "Great Soul," was an Indian hero and a political and spiritual leader. He adhered to the Hindu faith, as do I. Mahatma Gandhi used nonviolent resistance to win India's freedom. Mahatma Gandhi travelled to South Africa later that year to work there and saw that there was a lot of animosity toward Indians there. He started protesting because of this, and eventually he turned into a beloved figure to millions of people. Mahatma Gandhi is likely the only person, after the Buddha, who gives a measure of man's ability to nurture a rich inner life and achieve self-transformation. His life serves as an example of philosophy as the art of living. After the Buddha, Mahatma Gandhi is likely the only person who offers an indication of how far a person might develop a rich inner life and achieve self-transformation. How much of yourself can you change? How much internal change are you capable of making on your own, without assistance from any outside source, such as a guru?

"The main purpose of life is to live rightly, think rightly, and act rightly." "The soul must languish when we give all our thoughts to the body."
—Mahatma Gandhi

Mahatma Gandhi is a multifaceted individual who excels as a politician, social reformer, and mass leader. He serves as an example of developing oneself. Before leading the Indian liberation movement, he lived in South Africa to fight injustice and classism. Within ten years, Mahatma Gandhi had spread the Satyagraha school of thought and pushed the nation toward racial and social equality. Mahatma Gandhi had a first-class ticket, so he was placed in the first-class section. Since non-whites and "coolies" (a derogatory name for Indians) were not allowed in first-class compartments, a white individual who entered the cabin hurried to summon the white railway authorities, who ordered Mahatma Gandhi to transfer himself to the van compartment. Mahatma Gandhi objected and provided his ticket, but was told to leave politely or he would be forcibly removed. Mahatma Gandhi was forced out of the train and his luggage was thrown onto the platform when he refused to follow the officer's instructions. He became an activist to defend his rights as a result of this humiliation.

"What is success? I think it is a mixture of having a flair for the thing that you are doing; knowing that it is not enough, that you have got to have hard work and a certain sense of purpose."-Margaret Thatcher

The only Indian who was well-known worldwide was Mahatma Gandhi, who was the first to place India on the map of the world. He was the first Indian to get notoriety in politics, initially outside of India. He was the greatest mass mobilizer in Indian history, bringing millions of people into the public eye, particularly women. For a quarter of a century, he had such power over Indian politics that anybody who incurred his anger risked political suicide. He is the only leader in India, and maybe the whole globe, who has had an impact on so many facets of life and has something to say about each one, whether it be on issues of morality, sexuality, religion, the economy, or high politics.

"There is one quality which one must possess to win, and that is definiteness of purpose, the knowledge of what one wants, and a burning desire to possess it."- Napoleon Hill

Being an activist, he created the Satyagraha (truth-force) tactic, in which protesters participated in nonviolent marches and offered themselves up for arrest in opposition to unjust laws. In their early years of resistance to apartheid in South Africa, the African National Congress and the civil rights movement in the United States both benefited from this strategy. He was a thin man with a toothless grin, spectacles, and the traditional Hindu loincloth known as a dhoti. He also walked with a bamboo staff. He had the demeanour of a plain Hindu holy man. Mahatma Gandhi, however, confronted one of the mightiest empires in history with nothing more than remarkable courage and a steadfast dedication to peaceful resistance. Mahatma Gandhi fought against these injustices for 21 years.

"The only purpose for which power can be rightfully exercised over any member of a civilized community, against his will, is to prevent harm to others. His own good, either physical or moral, is not sufficient warrant."-John Stuart Mill

Martin Luther King Jr. formed his nonviolent ideology

during this time, which held that only nonviolent protests, like boycotts, marches, and sit-ins, could effect change. The American Baptist clergyman was a pioneer in the nation's Civil Rights Movement and a nonviolent campaigner. He organised the Montgomery bus boycott in 1955 and gave the possibly greatest speech in history, "I Have a Dream," in front of more than 250,000 people at the Washington, D.C., Civil Rights March in 1963. Mahatma Gandhi served as an influence on Martin Luther King Jr. when he was chosen to head the Montgomery bus boycott in Alabama in 1955. King would later remark that "India's Gandhi was the guiding light of our approach of nonviolent social change while the Montgomery boycott was ongoing." When the civil rights activist was training to become a minister, he first learned about Gandhi's nonviolent ideology.

"I refuse to accept the view that mankind is so tragically bound to the starless midnight of racism and war that the bright daybreak of peace and brotherhood can never become a reality... I believe that unarmed truth and unconditional love will have the final word."-Martin Luther King Jr.

King claimed that Gandhi provided him with "the way of social transformation I had been seeking" because of his capacity to effect change via love and nonviolence. King and his wife, Coretta Scott, King came to India after the boycott, which saw black residents of Montgomery refuse to board public transportation in an effort to denounce segregated seating, was successful. They visited the Gandhi family, even though Gandhi had already been slain at that point. When King returned to the United States, he continued to struggle for African Americans' equal rights using Gandhi's nonviolent tactics. Gandhi battled evil with the same zeal and strength as the violent resisters, but he did so out of love rather than hatred, according to King.

"We must develop and maintain the capacity to forgive. He who is devoid of the power to forgive is devoid of the power to love. There is some good in the worst of us and some evil in the best of us. When we discover this, we are less prone to hate our enemies."-Martin Luther King Jr.

Gandhi's Satyagraha campaign served as an inspiration for Mandela. It was a potent demonstration of passive resistance to injustice. This later served as motivation for the creation of the African National Congress and reaffirmed Mandela's faith in the universality of mankind. Mandela, who is sometimes referred to as the "Gandhi of South Africa," had close ties to India and traits in common with that country's "Father of the Nation." He was so impressed by Gandhi that he attributed Gandhi's philosophy to the success of South Africa's truth and reconciliation committee.

"What our origins are doesn't matter. What counts is where our qualities enable us to arrive."
-Nelson Mandela

Nelson Mandela a powerful voice of protest against injustice, a Gandhian at heart, a born leader for the underprivileged, a spirit of revolt against prejudice, and a warrior against the apartheid system, is a prime example of this. It would be pointless to attempt to summarise Nelson Mandela's life in an essay because it is so full of significant events. He is frequently referred to as the Mahatma Gandhi of South Africa because of his Gandhian-inspired human principles. Despite not having any roots in India, he had a close political relationship with Gandhi and the country. The Indian Eagle puts in a little effort to explore his relations with India and the Mahatma.

"There is no easy walk to freedom anywhere, and many of us will have to pass through the valley of the shadow of death again and again before we reach the mountaintop of our desires."- Nelson Mandela

Nelson Mandela was a revolutionary against apartheid who devoted his youth to the cause of African equality.He was imprisoned on Robben Island for life following violent protests, but was eventually released 27 years later. He spread lessons of forgiveness and equality after being freed. Mandela received the Nobel Peace Prize in 1993, and one year later he was elected as South Africa's first black president. Apartheid was finally ended in 1991.

"I learned that courage was not the absence of fear, but the triumph over it." – Nelson Mandela

One of the motivating factors behind Nelson Mandela's lifetime anti-apartheid fight was the Gandhian ideology. He looked up to Mahatma Gandhi as a leader. He was a devoted adherent of Gandhi's teachings on nonviolence and truth. Soon after his release from prison in 1990, he received the Bharat Ratna award. He was the country's highest civilian honor's first non-Indian recipient.

"I learned that courage was not the absence of fear, but the triumph over it. The brave man is not he who does not feel afraid, but he who conquers that fear."- Nelson Mandela

By summarising one of Nelson Mandela's remarks on Mahatma Gandhi, we want to demonstrate his passionate commitment to the latter. The Mahatma is an inseparable part of the African history of the movement against racism in South Africa, where he left an indelible influence of his unwavering determination in defiance of the wrong, in support of the right, and in pursuit of justice for the non-white, through his philosophy of truth and nonviolence, he said at the Gandhi Memorial's opening ceremony in South Africa in 1993.

Nelson Mandela maintained a positive relationship with India and Indian officials even after serving up to 27 years in jail for his opposition to the South African government's apartheid policy. For Indians of the twenty-first century, he is a very inspiring and magnificent character, comparable to the great sons of Mother India. Gandhi's teachings had a significant effect on both his political and non-political efforts to ensure peace and justice for black Africans, which earned him the 2001 International Gandhi Peace Prize.

"Our human compassion binds us the one to the other - not in pity or patronizingly, but as human beings who have learnt how to turn our common suffering into hope for the future."- Nelson Mandela

Nelson Mandela saw his trip to India as a religious pilgrimage. For this most famous opponent of apartheid, India was a country of principles and values. He visited Ahmedabad, where Gandhi had developed his nonviolent concept after returning to India from South Africa, where he had focused on his self-help ideas. In one of his addresses, Mandela claimed that he would never be able to live up to the standards of humanity, grandeur, and simplicity that the Mahatma had set through his own life's examples.

"Our prime purpose in this life is to help others. And if you can't help them, at least don't hurt them."
-Dalai Lama

The first and most crucial step in finding the solutions to how to lead a more fulfilling life is to have a clear knowledge of not just what you want your life to look like, but also how you truly want to live it. You are responsible for finding personal happiness, purpose, and satisfaction.

Finding your mission in life is similar to discovering anything new. People frequently seek to leap in with both feet when they become aroused. Finding meaning, though, requires more small steps. You will have more time to properly focus on what you want and what you can do to experience a sense of purpose if you go more slowly. As you move on, remember that you can depend on yourself to live each day to the fullest. Finding thankfulness is crucial for living a more fulfilling life, yet it may occasionally be challenging to find gratitude in the things around us. For this reason, it's crucial that you start out small on your path to living a life of meaning.

> *"To succeed in your mission, you must have*
> *single-minded devotion to your goal."*
> *-A. P. J. Abdul Kalam*

You too would see a glimpse of the endless options open to you if you looked through the same eyes. Be aware of the elements in your life to begin where you are. What you now own is the ideal basis for leading a prosperous life. Step away from your thoughts and into the vast ocean of your heart. Listen for the peace and clarity that may be found in the silent silence. The surge of inspiration he mentions is created by the energy and willpower he is referring to. Start from where you are, take the first step with faith, and have confidence that as long as you keep moving ahead, you will be led. Momentum conveys an enormous force that may outweigh difficulty and adversity. Starting from where you are right now, make a conscious decision to go forward with optimism and vigour, certain that life will guide you to where you need to be.

> *"Thousands of candles can be lighted from a single*
> *candle, and the life of the candle will not be shortened.*
> *Happiness never decreases by being shared." -Buddha*

Live in accordance with your values. Understanding what life, and especially your life, should feel like is one of the most crucial aspects of learning how to live a worthwhile existence. It could appear as though you are in a fog when you aren't being the real you. Despite being occupied, boredom still exists. You're rested, yet you're constantly worn out. Furthermore, even the smallest duties seem like an impossible burden. Living with purpose entails acting in accordance with your views and values and in a way that is consistent with how you feel. Although leading a purposeful life won't always result in a higher income, it will increase your desire to be a part of something greater than yourself. And the prize for doing so is inestimable.

"Outstanding people have one thing in common: an absolute sense of mission."

-Zig Ziglar

Setting mission has long been acknowledged as a potent strategy for raising our performance or behaviour. It may be quite effective in launching and directing us along a more meaningful and rewarding road when we apply the same method to discovering objectives for our own life. Knowing what you truly want to accomplish in life may often be the hardest part of setting life goals. We may have hazy concepts or just be unsure of where to go for them. But having attainable and meaningful life objectives may help us get a new perspective and, more significantly, can make us happier and more pleased with our lives. The desirable states that people want to achieve, maintain, or avoid are known as life goals. Simply expressed, these objectives are things we wish to achieve or complete in our life. They are usually more significant and connected to our true selves.

"By letting it go it all gets done. The world is won by those who let it go. But when you try and try, the world is beyond winning." — Lao Tzu

Any initiative to forge a bond of purpose must be grounded on a social contract of faith in our people. Any drive for purpose will be seen as just another paper exercise, or worse, a cunning strategy to use our people as a means to an end without the society ultimately caring about them as people, if we have not consistently communicated that we care and that our people matter, and if we have not acted in a way that is consistent with this. Such actions will only serve to further dehumanise our staff members and distance them from our goal of establishing a feeling of community.On the other hand, if our actions are perceived as coming from a leadership that genuinely cares about acting in the best interests of its employees and the business, it will inspire a wave of goodwill that will advance us toward our shared goal of fulfilling that shared purpose.

"A mission statement is not something you write overnight... But fundamentally, your mission statement becomes your constitution, the solid expression of your vision and values. It becomes the criterion by which you measure everything else in your life. "
-Stephen Covey

CHAPTER SIX

Unleash Your True Potential

"Once you have mastered time, you will understand how true it is that most people overestimate what they can accomplish in a year--and underestimate what they can achieve in a decade!" --Tony Robbins

You were born with exceptional talents and abilities.

Many individuals underrate their potential and what they are capable of. The gap between where we are now and our potential is what we call potential. Potential frequently results in success for that person. This is not always about success (although for many, this is exactly what it is). Finding tranquilly is important to some people. Some people place more value on "being" than on "having" or "doing." Others care more about relationships and having the freedom to be themselves in order to meet the appropriate partner. Some claim that if we need to "unleash your potential," it suggests that something is wrong with us or that we are insufficient just as we are.

"Life is full of beauty. Notice it. Notice the bumble bee, the small child, and the smiling faces. Smell the rain, and feel the wind. Live your life to the fullest potential, and fight for your dreams."-Ashley Smith

Unleashing Potential, in my opinion, is about helping individuals realise their ambitions and aspirations, no matter what they may be, starting from where they are right now. It involves freeing individuals from the things that are preventing them from leading the life they desire and assisting in putting them in a position to succeed, whatever that may entail for them. You are incredibly capable and have all it takes to live the life of your dreams.

"God, our Creator, has stored within our minds and personalities, great potential strength and ability. Prayer helps us tap and develop these powers."-A. P. J. Abdul Kalam

Whether you are aware of it or not, you were born with exceptional talents and abilities. The narrative of your life is how you use it for your benefit and the benefit of others. Will this story help you realise your potential? Let's see if you can get things going! You are the only person in the world who truly understands how you feel. Let's face it. Others may make assumptions, conjectures, or inquiries, but they can never be certain.

"Never underestimate the power of dreams and the influence of the human spirit. We are all the same in this notion: The potential for greatness lives within each of us."-Wilma Rudolph

Abraham Maslow, a psychologist, used the term "actualization" to describe reaching our highest potential and being everything we may be. The effect is the second element. As we grow older, we must give the world the finest versions of ourselves in order to positively influence others and impact their lives. It's important because, for the majority of us, our purpose eventually has to be connected to something greater than ourselves. An example of a higher reason may be our family's or friends' happiness, a greater goal to change society in some way, or our religious adherence to a transcendent deity.

"There will always be obstacles and challenges that stand in your way. Building mental strength will help you develop resilience to those potential hazards so you can continue on your journey to success."- Amy Morin

The power you possess is something you yourself are unaware of. You may use your strength to get what you deserve in life by focusing all of your energy in the appropriate directions. You must use the power inside you to do it. Most of the time, you concentrate on difficulties rather than what may go well. You should perform a few rituals in order to focus your energies in the direction of your dreams. You may employ your entire potential and become alive by engaging in these rituals. We underrate our capacity to do more in life.

"Too often we underestimate the power of a touch, a smile, a kind word, a listening ear, an honest compliment, or the smallest act of caring, all of which have the potential to turn a life around."- Leo Buscaglia

We don't reach our full potential. Once you start using your power, you'll notice that your life is shifting toward far better and more fulfilling experiences. Your world is shaped by your thoughts. Your life is governed in part by your ideas. Take care of your thoughts. Our minds are quite strong. It complies with the directives we give it. That guidance is nothing more than our ideas. It will never operate at its best if we feed it doubt. Don't let small-minded and pessimistic thoughts limit your possibilities.

Your beliefs are formed by your ideas.

"In life, it is important to not be afraid to put yourself out there, win or lose. It is all about the spirit of challenging yourself to be open to realizing your highest potential."- Cynthia Bailey

A wonderful method to drive activity is by setting goals. It gives your following steps direction and helps to clear your mind. Goals that are challenging encourage the flow state that so many people want. Some people like to remark that "a life without challenge and danger is not worth living." Setting engaging, difficult, yet manageable goals is the secret to unlocking potential. The objective may be written down and spoken aloud. You need an alternative aim if it didn't inspire or move you, if you weren't motivated to act or weren't sure what to do. As Lao-Tzu once stated, "A journey of a thousand miles begins with a single step." To fully realise your potential, this is also true. Quickly assess your talents and limitations, identify the world's hunger you can alleviate, and establish ambitious goals for yourself. Then, use each day to take one tiny step in the right direction.

"God puts people in our lives on purpose so we can help them succeed and help them become all He created them to be. Most people will not reach their full potential without somebody else believing in them."- Joel Osteen

We make millions of decisions every day, most of them unconsciously. Your life is the total of all these choices, both small and large. For this reason, developing good behaviour is crucial. You could learn how to be grateful, manage stress, and have wholesome, motivating relationships. You might also discover how to change bad habits into good ones. Although they won't change overnight, once developed, they will have a favourable influence on hundreds of your judgments in the future.Resentment is one of the main causes of not reaching your full potential. "Resentment is like swallowing poison and waiting for the other person to die," Malachy McCourt once said.

"Don't let other people influence your life to think negatively. Concentrate on the now since the past is over and the future is uncertain. Let the past not determine your future."

Our sensitivity grows directly in proportion to how well we react to our impressions. Your awareness of the good things in your life will increase if you are grateful. You'll be more relaxed, you'll notice more opportunities, and your relationships will get better.

"Everybody has a creative potential and from the moment you can express this creative potential, you can start changing the world."-Paulo Coelho

Since this is the only life you have, I hope you fully realise all of your potential. I think you can do great things if you know what you have, understand how you can use it, let go of the painful past, and develop good habits over the daily steps you take. What would you do if you were not afraid? What if there were no boundaries that you had built for yourself in your life to unleash your potential ? What if your life's scrapes and bruises vanished, giving you the confidence to move forward?

What if you set down those bulky bags of useless items you're holding on to?

Instead of being discouraged by the possibility of anything going wrong, what if you were inspired by what might be? Is it okay if you refuse to accept "I'll get by"?

- *How would it feel to put your own pleasure ahead of your concerns about what other people think of you? What if you began to look forward to the journey rather than rushing to the end point just to be disappointed?*
- *If you had the opportunity to create the screenplay for this thing we call life, how would you do it?*
- *What if the love you long for was always present inside of you but you were too busy or frightened to feel it?*
- *What if the greatest danger of all is actually that you don't live the life you want to live?*

"Continuous effort, not strength or intelligence is the key to unlocking our potential."-Winston Churchill

Your life is shaped by your beliefs. God has given each of us a special gift that is vast. However, we somehow fail to put it to use, and we go through life with false notions and unpleasant emotions. But you can always alter your thought process. Switch your negative ideas with optimistic ones. It works miracles. To reach your maximum potential, you must alter your ideas.

"We attempt to improve the outside world when we are in distress. But the truth is that we should pay attention to our inner selves and ideas."

We have no control over the events or circumstances, but we do have power over our thoughts. Your beliefs are formed by your ideas. Your ideas are everything that makes up your beliefs. And your life is governed by your beliefs, whether they are false or true. The definition of believe, according to the dictionary, is an acceptance that something exists or is true, particularly one without proof.

"Impossible is just a word thrown around by small men who find it easier to live in the world they've been given than to explore the power they have to change it. Impossible is not a fact. It's an opinion. Impossible is potential. Impossible is temporary. Impossible is nothing."
– Muhammad Ali

Your life is hampered by these ideas. One must strengthen his mind if he wants to succeed. Never let your mind wander to unpleasant ideas. The first step you should take if you want to live the life of your dreams and achieve your objectives is to change your mindset from one of negativity and mediocrity to one of optimism and greatness. Your ideas have the potential to affect not only you but also other people. Because life is so brief, there's no use in doing something you'll later regret.

"You measure the size of the accomplishment by the obstacles you have to overcome to reach your goals." -
Booker T. Washington

You work at your highest capacity when you are doing what you love. This ultimately results in success and a happy life. There isn't a unique recipe for this. Those who are aware of this enjoy happy lives. Do you only get a job to get a paycheck? Are we only here to work, pay our bills, and pass away? Is that right? NoWe're all here to have happy lives. We are here to pursue our passions. Everything will come into your life naturally when you are doing what you love.

"Some failure in life is inevitable. It is impossible to live without failing at something, unless you live so cautiously that you might as well not have lived at all -- in which case, you fail by default." - J.K. Rowling

You'll be prosperous, wealthy, and well-known. Our mental and emotional health improves when we are engaged in what we enjoy. Your time and life are not worth living to please others. You are here to gratify yourself, not other people. Do what you love. What occurs if your mother prepares the food you adore? Without her extending an invitation to join her at the table, you quickly grab it. You smell it first, then you see how it looks. As you begin to eat, use all of your senses. Your true strength comes from doing what you enjoy without regard for what others may think of you.

"Never give up. Today is hard, tomorrow will be worse, but the day after tomorrow will be sunshine." - Jack Ma

Change is a necessary part of life in order to fully realise our potential. "You simply have to accept things as they are and take no action." Given that our whole focus is on creating it, it is most likely the greatest discipline in the world. The key is to be present and trust the process. In the same vein, concentrate on what matters and let the rest go away. You don't have to take on more than is necessary at the moment. In actuality, doing less frequently produces better outcomes. A recycled thinking awareness is expressed through popular culture. If you want to fit in, there is a place for you, and you don't have to struggle to get there.

"You don't learn to walk by following the rules. You learn by doing, and falling over." - Richard Branson

Go out on a limb where the fruit is more rewarding if you want to be a thinker, a rebel, an innovator, an optimist, or a creative person, though. The world urges you to take chances. While some approaches encourage you to experience yourself with increased zest, those risks may or may not pay off. When we honour our actual nature rather than engaging in an internal conflict that we will ultimately lose, we can achieve the state of mind . Our determination to calm the turbulent thoughts in our heads so that the stillness can resonate throughout us leads to an effortless life. Lao Tzu tells us that when we synchronise with life's flow, everything—not just certain things, but all things, including the life we aspire to live—succeeds.

"The people who are crazy enough to think they can change the world are the ones who do." - Steve Jobs

We must begin acting in ways we haven't necessarily done previously if we want to gain confidence, and some of those ways will unavoidably be uncomfortable. People discuss what is comfortable and what is uncomfortable in conventional coaching and psychology. They'll say things like, "Everything you already have and do is inside your comfort zone, and everything you want is outside of it." They are not incorrect, but they are oversimplifying the situation and omitting a critical component. It sounds as though any place outside of your comfort zone will be uncomfortable when you say you only have to step outside of it to acquire what you want. But isn't that not the case? There is a slight distinction between viewing a snake safely contained in a glass tank via a pet store window and falling into a snake pit if you wish to overcome your fear of snakes.

"A person should set his goals as early as he can and devote all his energy and talent to getting there. With enough effort, he may achieve it. Or he may find something that is even more rewarding. But in the end, no matter what the outcome, he will know he has been alive." - Walt Disney

Constantly comparing oneself to others is one of the most prevalent ways people lose their confidence without even recognising it. And since you're enrolled in this course, which implies that you must be educated and tolerant, I'm willing to wager that you even have a tendency to do that. However, you're generally only comparing yourself to individuals you perceive as the greatest or most outstanding people in your immediate environment.

> *"The ones who, in your subconscious, you believe are somehow superior to or more successful than you in some way. You then judge yourself because you aren't as good at it as they are because you compare yourself to what they do that you think they are so amazing at."*

However, if you were as good at it as they are, you wouldn't be comparing yourself to them but rather to someone who is even more skilled than they are. Nearly everyone engages in this. The real kicker is here. Most of the time, we also greatly underrate the people to whom we are making these comparisons. We only see what they want us to see, and whatever we see is impacted by our preconceived notions of them, which are frequently incorrect.

"The future rewards those who press on. I don't have time to feel sorry for myself. I don't have time to complain. I'm going to press on." - Barack Obama

There is a phenomenon in psychology known as the halo effect. The halo effect, put simply, is the propensity for individuals to confuse one favourable feature with another. As a result, when we meet someone who appears intelligent, for instance, we also often think that they are amusing, kind, or possess any other trait we place a high value on. And although it's not always true, we have a tendency to think that successful deals are synonymous with success.

Any individual who has achieved great success has failed, sometimes on a huge, humiliating scale. Stop being scared to put in the effort and fail, because no one who is successful will ever condemn you for it. Only those who have never failed themselves will ever condemn you, generally because they have made extremely safe decisions. Face your concerns, quit being frightened of failing, and go with the task at hand. Putting in the effort is how you develop bravery and start moving in the direction of being your best self.

"Do the one thing you think you cannot do. Fail at it. Try again. Do better the second time. The only people who never tumble are those who never mount the high wire. This is your moment. Own it." - Oprah Winfrey

You are sad because you are not realising your potential or attaining your ambitions. First of all, be aware that you are not alone; this occurs to everyone. You are capable of improving. It will take a lot of effort, bravery, and grit, but if you persevere and have faith in yourself, you will succeed in your endeavours and become the finest version of yourself. Instead of spending more time working on a project that requires attention, going to the gym, preparing supper at home, etc., it would be nice to unwind, watch a movie or a show, meet a friend for dinner, etc.

"If you're not stubborn, you'll give up on experiments too soon. And if you're not flexible, you'll pound your head against the wall and you won't see a different solution to a problem you're trying to solve." - Jeff Bezos

Therefore, when we seek out others to contrast ourselves with, we don't just tend to seek out those we believe to be superior to us in some way; rather, once we find one quality in them that we would rate higher than our own, the halo effect takes over and leads us to believe that they possess a multitude of qualities superior to our own, whether or not that is actually the case. And now is the time to begin executing both of those actions.

> *"The best way to achieve it, though, is to choose the appropriate person to compare oneself to in the first place, as it is extremely difficult to manage cognitive biases like the halo effect."*

In any case, there is only one person to whom we should be compared. And that is who we were before. Because the only way to determine whether your progress is being made is to compare where you are right now to where you wanted to be one week, one month, or one year ago.

It's excellent that you're closer; keep up the good effort. If you're not, you'll need to either start working or switch to a different type of employment that is more effective. In any case, there is only one person to whom we should be compared. And that is who we were before. Because the only way to determine whether your progress is being made is to compare where you are right now to where you wanted to be one week, one month, or one year ago. It's excellent that you're closer; keep up the good effort. If you're not, you'll need to either start working or switch to a different type of employment that is more effective.

"The question I ask myself like almost every day is, 'Am I doing the most important thing I could be doing?'" - Mark Zuckerberg

The best of the best, the top performers, act in this manner for three straightforward reasons. They don't worry about what other people are doing. They understand that their personal outcomes don't have to be influenced by those of others. And they are aware that continuing to develop from where they are now is the only way to enhance their outcomes.

You will experience an immediate and long-lasting boost in your confidence once you stop comparing yourself to other people and begin comparing yourself to your previous self while working on living in your growth zone, developing your super ego, and mastering the other techniques and philosophies from this course. Here is your straightforward workout. Every week, set aside a specific day and time to sit down and spend a few minutes comparing your present self to your past self. Note your current position in relation to where you were a month, six months, or a year ago.

- *What steps have you taken to get closer to your objectives?*
- *What part of your life has changed?*

The answers you discover should indicate what you need to do more of to get the desired results. The secret is to identify your strengths so you can capitalise on them. Frederick Buechner, a theologian, once observed that "your calling is where your passions meet the needs of the world."

"I think goals should never be easy, they should force you to work, even if they are uncomfortable at the time." -
Michael Phelps

It is a good idea to consider how you may use your skills and limitations to better the world if you are aware of them. Asking your friends and coworkers to name your five strengths and one flaw might be all that is required. The second important question you must ask yourself is, "How can I develop in these areas?" People typically regret the things they did not do rather than the ones they did when they are facing death. There are many difficulties and anxieties in life, but you may ask yourself a few questions: When I'm older, would I regret not doing this? Will I still remember this in ten years? How important is it to me? If I don't do this, will I be able to look in the mirror? You must have courage to realise your potential; otherwise, you will end up going in circles.

"You can only become truly accomplished at something you love. Don't make money your goal. Instead, pursue the things you love doing, and then do them so well that people can't take their eyes off you." - Maya Angelou

I would begin any of these undertakings in the same way. However, following these procedures alone won't help; you also need mentors, in-depth knowledge, and practise time. The learning curve for one of these initiatives will be severe until you figure it out and can really make things happen. People often wait for a better chance, a better opportunity, or a better occasion in life—a future moment when the universe will align perfectly. When this day eventually arrives, you will feel prepared to take immediate action. However, the day won't come unless you decide that it will.

"To live a fulfilled life, we need to keep creating the "what is next", of our lives. Without dreams and goals there is no living, only merely existing, and that is not why we are here." - Mark Twain

CHAPTER SEVEN

Finding Your Inner Peace

The secret to inner serenity is healthy emotional flow.

"The life of inner peace, being harmonious and without stress, is the easiest type of existence." —Norman Vincent Peale

Every aspect of your life, including how you see and express the world and yourself, will alter when you are essentially joyful and do not need to do anything to be happy. You won't have any vested interests anymore since you will already be joyful by nature, regardless of what you do or don't do, what you receive or don't get, what occurs or doesn't happen.

"If you are depressed you are living in the past if you are anxious you are living in the future, if you are at peace, you are living in the present." —Lao Tzu

When you are naturally joyful, everything you do will change significantly. The first and most important duty of a person is to develop into a joyful being. The most important thing in life is not to be happy. It is a basic component of life. What else can you do with your life if you're not happy? Only when you are content will big opportunities present themselves.

"Do not let the behavior of others destroy your inner peace." —Dalai Lama

You will only spread your inner excellence through all you do. It doesn't matter how you feel about it; that is the truth. You cannot contribute significantly to the world until something of actual significance occurs within you. Therefore, the first thing you must do if you are worried about the world is to change into a joyful being.

"Nobody can bring you peace but yourself." —Ralph Waldo Emerson

No matter what you are chasing in life—whether it's money, influence, education, or service—you are doing it because you have a deep-seated belief that it will make you happy. Because it is our innate nature, every action we take in this world stems from a desire to be happy. You were just content when you were a youngster. That is who you are. You are the source of your own joy, and you can control it.

"You should feel beautiful and you should feel safe. What you surround yourself with should bring you peace of mind and peace of spirit." —Stacy London

Live for your family, not for your legacy. The creation of a legacy is ineffective as a goal. Generations tend to remember those who put their family before themselves. Discover your passion. Howard Thurman, a philosopher, once stated, "Don't inquire what the world needs. Find out what gives you life, then go do it.

"It isn't enough to talk about peace. One must believe in it. And it isn't enough to believe in it. One must work at it." —Eleanor Roosevelt

People who have come alive are what the world needs. Put off immediate enjoyment in favour of long-term fulfilment. We put a lot of effort into teaching this to our kids, but after that, we stop applying the lesson to ourselves. Is it truly worth going into debt now for a $50,000 automobile if it means you won't have the money for your son's education tomorrow? Do you value the joy of a well-timed sarcastic jab more than the potential damage it can do to a relationship? Is this one-night stand a suitable replacement for a lifetime of dedication? to bolster other individuals.

"Peace is a daily, a weekly, a monthly process, gradually changing opinions, slowly eroding old barriers, quietly building new structures." —John F. Kennedy

Did you notice how beautifully the sun rose this morning? The flowers grew, no stars fell, and the galaxies are in excellent working order. Every detail is in place. Even when everything in the universe is working out splendidly today, a single idea that keeps running through your brain causes you to think that everything is going wrong. The main reason why suffering exists is that the majority of people no longer understand what this life is all about. To put it bluntly, you have elevated your little product above the work of the Creator by making their psychological process far more significant than their existential process.

"Peace is a journey of a thousand miles and it must be taken one step at a time." -Lyndon B. Johnson

The main cause of all this pain is that The full meaning of what it means to be alive here has escaped us.Your current experience is a result of a thought you are currently having or an emotion you are currently experiencing. Additionally, your thoughts and feelings might not even be related to the constrained reality of your life. The production as a whole is going great, yet one one idea or feeling has the power to wreck the whole thing.

"Peace brings with it so many positive emotions that it is worth aiming for in all circumstances." -Estella Eliot

Every day, ask yourself, "What can I do to inspire my wife, my children, my coworkers, my friends, etc." Be a person of honour. What's superior to money? Your standing What lasts longer than fame? Your honesty What is more likely to be discussed in the future than how awesome your automobile was? The dignity and honour of the person, who, for all they know, may have ridden a bus to work every day. Instead of focusing on receiving, live your life by giving. To be remembered, you don't have to be a wealthy benefactor with your name on a wall. Give what you have; do what you can.

" Peace cannot be kept by force. It can only be achieved by understanding." -Albert Einstein

Many famous businesspeople, like Bill Gates, Steve Jobs, and Marc Zuckerberg, succeeded at a relatively young age. Although you would believe they were handed a magic formula for success, the fact is that they gave up something in order to be successful. In truth, success requires a lot of sacrifices. It's hardly news that excellence necessitates sacrifice. Any thriving businessman will tell you that getting to the top isn't an easy journey taken in a plush Porsche. Instead, there are things you must give up in order to have a better future, which frequently involves losing your girlfriend or your BMW.

"Imagine all the people living life in peace. You may say that I'm a dreamer, but I'm not the only one. I hope someday you'll join us and the world will be as one." —John Lennon

Make your social media feeds uplifting and joyful. Once you've finished unfollowing those bad influencers, go on to find some good ones. Look around to see if you can find any influencers who are doing something that you would truly support. Follow organisations, causes, and activists working to advance body positivity, sustainability, equality, and other causes.

> *"Make sure your feed is balanced between things that will make you feel better or give you more confidence and ones that will motivate you to improve yourself or the world. Set time limits for using social media."*

You shouldn't spend hours reading over your social media pages just because they are now encouraging spaces. It's time to start comparing using social media to eating processed food or engaging in harmful habits in general.

"Peace is not absence of conflict, it is the ability to handle conflict by peaceful means." —Ronald Reagan

What you refer to as "my mind" is not genuinely yours. You lack independent thought. Please take a close look. What you refer to as "my thoughts" is only the trash heap of civilization. Every person who passes you in the street shoves something into your skull. You actually don't have a choice in terms of who you choose to receive from and who you don't. You will get a lot more from someone if you tell them, "I don't like this individual," than from anybody else. Really, there isn't much of a choice. This trash is helpful if you know how to process and use it.

"Not one of us can rest, be happy, be at home, be at peace with ourselves, until we end hatred and division."
-John Lewis

You can only use this collection of perceptions and knowledge to help you survive in the world. Nothing is connected to what you are. As I just said, you simply have to realise that your thoughts and feelings are unimportant if you wish to enter into existential reality. Reality has nothing to do with what you believe. It doesn't really apply to daily life. The mind is simply babbling unfounded information that you have learned elsewhere. If you believe it to be significant, you won't search elsewhere. Your focus will naturally go toward whatever you value most. Your entire attention will be focused there if your thoughts and feelings are significant. That, however, is a psychological fact. That is unrelated to anything existential.

"When you make peace with yourself, you make peace with the world." -Maha Ghosananda

While occasionally indulging in fatty or sugary foods is acceptable, eating them for three meals a day, every day, will be detrimental to your physical health. Similar to this, see social media as something that should be used sparingly to avoid damaging your mental health. Stop spending time with people who bring you down or limit you.

"Love and peace of mind do protect us. They allow us to overcome the problems that life hands us. They teach us to survive... to live now... to have the courage to confront each day." -Bernie Siegel

Nowadays, social media plays a significant role in many of our lives, but the actual people you spend time with are far more significant. Or they ought to be, really. Make a choice to spend less time with people who are a bad influence in your life, who are always depressing you or preventing you from reaching your potential. If your efforts to talk with them about it have met with resistance, While you shouldn't desert a friend who is going through a difficult time, it's definitely a good idea to rethink how much time you spend with individuals who routinely affect you negatively.

"To seek out your own inner Peace is the greatest gift you could ever hope to give to this world." – Eric Walton

Generous lives leave enduring imprints on history. Be genuine. Talk honestly with your husband, open up to your kids, and be open with your friends. Men who erect barriers around their hearts and souls are forgotten because no one has ever met them. narrates the tales. If we won't allow ourselves to be recognised, how can we hope to be remembered? Cherish your family. Do you think this is a no-brainer? Well, a lot of us could benefit from a love primer. It is not rude, self-centered, irritable, or keeps track of wrongdoings.

"Inner peace can be reached only when we practice forgiveness. Forgiveness is letting go of the past, and is therefore the means for correcting our misperceptions."
-Gerald G. Jampolsky

Love rejoices in the truth rather than taking pleasure in wickedness. It always defends, always believes, always aspires, and always endures. Create a celebration-focused culture in your household. Be like the family who celebrates the 100th anniversary of their great-grandparents' arrival in America or the couple who sends cards to each other on the occasion of their first date, engagement, or closing on their first house.

"You'll never find peace of mind until you listen to your heart." -George Michael

Be the family that commemorates milestones, anniversaries, memories, and historical events. "Be a champion for what you believe in, and then let your convictions direct your course of action." Find a mistake and fix it. Perhaps your truly big contribution is still to come. Become an advocate for your beliefs, and then let them direct your course of action. The unexamined existence, according to Socrates, is not worth living. Perhaps as a result of some introspection, your legacy will become apparent.

"Having inner peace means committing to letting go of self-criticism and self-doubt."-Sanaya Roman

Millions of people who slept yesterday are still asleep today, while you and I are still awake. Isn't it wonderful that you're awake? So be happy that you got up. Next, take a peek around, and if you see somebody, give them a grin. Someone close to so many people did not get out of bed this morning. Wow! Everyone you care about woke up. Isn't today wonderful? Then step outside and observe the trees. Last night, they also did not pass away.

"Mindset is everything. Like the eye of a storm -find the sunshine and calm within you, even if there is chaos outside of you." -Brittany Burgunder

Although you may find this absurd, you will understand its truth when a loved one fails to awaken. Don't wait till then to appreciate its worth. Knowing that you are alive and that everything that matters to you is alive is the most valuable thing. It is not anything absurd. So many people did not wake up on this terrible night, including the loved ones of so many others. Isn't it a wonderful occasion? At least smile and express appreciation. Get better at loving a few people.

"Life is a series of natural and spontaneous changes. Don't resist them; that only creates sorrow. Let reality be reality. Let things flow naturally forward in whatever way they like." -Lao Tzu

Today, we are pursuing happiness with such fervour that the planet's basic existence is in danger. Don't try to find happiness. Understand how to share your delight with others. When you look back on your life, the most beautiful times in it are when you are experiencing joy, not when you are trying to find it. Your quality will never be what you save. Your quality is seen in what you give out. If you hold on to your happiness, nobody will hold you accountable after you pass away. The first thing you should do when you get up is smile. To whom? No one. Because it's not a minor thing that you woke up at all.

It is not based on what you possess. Depending on how they are at the time. The majority of people suffer, not because of what they lack. Simply said, it's because they are making comparisons between themselves and others. You make yourself sad because you are riding a motorcycle and you notice someone driving a Mercedes. He sees you on a motorcycle and thinks of it as a limousine for a person on a bicycle. When someone sees the bicycle while strolling down the street, they may think, "Wow, what I would have done with my life if I simply had that!" It is a pointless game that never ends.

"Each one has to find his peace from within. And peace to be real must be unaffected by outside circumstances." — Mahatma Gandhi

The way you dress, your educational background, your family history, or the amount of money you have in the bank right now do not affect the quality of your life. The quality of your life is determined by how content and joyful you are from within. All those individuals will never experience genuine joy in their life since they rely on other people's actions to make them happy. It is surely time for us to examine how to cultivate our own wellness.

"When you've seen beyond yourself, then you may find, peace of mind is waiting there." – George Harrison

You can plainly understand from your own life experience that altering your interiority is the only way for you to truly find wellbeing. If you rely on the outside world to make you happy, you need to realise that things outside of your control rarely go exactly as you would like them to. When this is the case, at least one person—you—must have your desires fulfilled. The obvious answer would be delight if things turned out the way you wanted them to. There is no doubt that someone who lacks food and other essentials for living may suffer physically. That requires attention. We must address such issues first for these individuals. However, the majority of people have a never-ending list of requirements. Do you believe the person operating the vehicle is happier than the person crossing the street? You're under no obligation to pursue that. Joy is the only state you can be in if you revert to your true nature.

"You have to grow from the inside out. None can teach you, none can make you spiritual. There is no other teacher but your own soul." -Swami Vivekananda

CHAPTER EIGHT

Leave Your Comfort Zone

"Your work is going to fill a large part of your life, and the only way to be truly satisfied is to do what you believe is great work. And the only way to do great work is to love what you do. If you haven't found it yet, keep looking. Don't settle. As with all matters of the heart, you'll know when you find it." --Steve Jobs

The beginning of life is beyond your comfort zone.

Why are so many of us scared to leave our comfort zones, although it has long been believed that life begins at the other end? I'll tell you why: being in your comfort zone reduces worry and tension. This makes it quite simple to never cross the line since, let's face it, being in your own safety bubble is pretty darn comfortable.

Some people find it impossible to imagine leaving their safety bubble, especially if you are confident that you will experience anxiety. Having said that, we all occasionally need a little more incentive to face our fears and leave the safety of our comfort zones.

"As you move outside of your comfort zone, what was once the unknown and frightening becomes your new normal." -Robin S. Sharma

Discover your comfort zone, then unwind for a while. Once you've changed your challenge to something more manageable and within your growth range, try it again. Now, when you're in your growth zone, you might occasionally experience some uneasy feelings, but they'll be a lot easier to handle. These emotions may include apprehension, mild anxiety, discomfort, stress, and even a small amount of fear. And that's totally okay. It's not your intention to never feel these emotions.

"The comfort zone is nothing else but a graveyard for your dreams & ideas." -Anonymous

Getting comfortable doing what you should or need to do in spite of them is your goal. To put it another way, you want to get used to being a little uncomfortable. The wonderful thing is that after some time spent in your growth zone, your subconscious mind, which was previously serving up all kinds of anxious, stressed-out, or apprehensive thinking, starts to recognise that you are completely safe. And when it does, it alters those beliefs and begins to give you thoughts about what you're doing that are relaxed, secure, confident, or even happy and excited.

"Alter begins at the end of your comfort zone; you never change your life until you move out of your comfort zone. Instead of telling ourselves lies and making up reasons to stay in our comfort zones, we must be honest about what we want and take risks."

So, as you can see, this is not how the comfort zone is modelled. It extends beyond the inside and outside. In order to master the skill of leaving our comfort zone in healthy and beneficial ways, there are two additional zones that we should be aware of. Because some actions that are outside of our comfort zone—like falling into a pit of snakes—are so far from it, taking them will induce psychological distress.

"You can choose courage or you can choose comfort. You cannot have both." -Brene Brown

Additionally, after going through anything painful, we often try to avoid it in the future. These things fall into what we call the panic zone, and entering the panic zone can cause us to withdraw from an activity or a circumstance to the point where we give up on ever mastering it. What, therefore, should we do instead?

"The hardest thing to do is leaving your comfort zone. But you have to let go of the life you're familiar with and take the risk to live the life you dream about." -T. Arigo

Your comfort zone begins to enlarge as a result and catches up with you. And as a result, the activities you were doing outside of your comfort zone will now move inside of it. And everything changes when that occurs. As you can see, your comfort zone and your panic zone have a predetermined relationship. This implies that the panic zone is pushed farther out when your comfort zone grows to incorporate anything new.

"By leaving your comfort zone behind and taking a leap of faith into something new, you find out who you are truly capable of becoming." -Anonymous

This allows you to start practising and mastering things that were previously in your panic zone and have them slide into your growth zone. And as you continue to do so, more and more items will inevitably migrate from your growth zone into your comfort zone, which will eventually include everything you want to feel secure and at ease about. That sounds good, doesn't it?

"We have to be honest about what we want and take risks rather than lie to ourselves and make excuses to stay in our comfort zone." -Ray Bennett

Making your own growth zone workouts is a fantastic way to build your confidence, acquire new knowledge, and increase your experience. And you may start doing that in whichever parts of your life you'd like by adhering to the straightforward procedures I'm about to share with you. The first step is to pick an area of your life where you want to gain more confidence. Create activities that get harder and harder in stage two. They should span the gamut from the most important thing you want to feel secure doing in the future to what you can do now if you just push yourself a little bit. After that, in step three, you begin working out in your growth zone. You repeat the process once the exercises become simple enough.

"If it doesn't challenge you, it doesn't change you."
-Anonymous

When you do, you'll notice that some of the exercises that were once in your panic zone are now ones you can start working on in the growth zone. And one of those things will eventually be the major task you want to feel confident completing. Pretty basic, yes? Let's now have a look at an illustration of what that may entail. Let's assume that Umesh wishes to gain more confidence when speaking in front of groups so that he can contribute to meetings, make presentations, or lead seminars.

"True self-discovery begins where your comfort zone ends." -Adam Braun

Today, though, Umesh finds it difficult to even speak in meetings if there are more than a few attendees. Umesh's actions in this scenario might resemble these. He states that his first goal is to feel comfortable speaking in front of a sizable crowd. He develops some exercise suggestions in phase two. When someone in a huge group says something he agrees with, one thing he believes he can start doing today is to start saying "yeah" and "I agree" in a clear and concise manner.

"A ship is always safe at the shore-but that is not what it is built for." -Albert Einstein

Asking simple questions in those bigger groups, such as "Can you repeat that?", is one that could be a bit more difficult but that he believes he can do at least occasionally. The task of creating and giving a brief, one-to three-minute presentation could be just on the other side of his panic zone. It's likely that the concept of spending one minute presenting anything to the group has slid just inside of Umesh's Growth Zone after he becomes confident in both stating his yeses and asking his questions. Now, keep in mind that Umesh could occasionally want to back out of performing these workouts. That's quite natural, and our superego—which we'll talk about in the next video—usually produces it. But as long as he can continue the practise despite these emotions, despite the superego, and without inducing a panic attack, he will eventually succeed in his endeavour.

"Resistance to change is very much governed by your comfort zone. Just because something is comfortable does not for a moment mean it's what you want, or even good for you for that matter." -Robin H-C

We begin to step outside of our comfort zone and gain confidence when we take action despite feeling anxious or stressed out. You have to go through this process for yourself and come up with at least one activity that you can perform later today or tomorrow as your workout for this chapter. There is no need to hold off. You'll get where you want to go more quickly if you begin to build your confidence as soon as possible.

"Coming out of your comfort zone is tough in the beginning, chaotic in the middle, and awesome in the end...because in the end, it shows you a whole new world."
-Manoj Arora

Step outside your comfort zone and give something new a try. It might be something little, like trying a new meal, picking up a new hobby, or changing your bus route; or it can be something huge, like studying in a different area, picking up a new skill, or going to a foreign nation that you've never been to. Make your room a place you enjoy being in. The same for your workstation at work. Get rid of everything that is impeding your productivity. It should be surrounded by things that motivate and encourage you.

"No one likes to move beyond their comfort zone, but as the saying goes, that's where the magic happens. It's where we grow, learn, and develop in a way that expands our horizons beyond what we thought was possible." -Andy Molinsky

Each of us has a dream identity that we aspire to. What would your ideal self do? How can you begin to be your ideal self right away? You can do considerably more with the help of role models than you can on your own. Oprah Winfrey has personally inspired me due to the millions of lives she has touched, among other things. They inspire me to reach new heights because what I see in them and what they accomplish serves as a reminder of who I am and what I am capable of.

"Face the fear, even if it's only a tiptoe outside of your comfort zone instead of a leap. Progress is progress."
-Annette White

Having someone work with you on your objectives is the only way to progress more quickly. They'll not only inspire you to work harder, but they'll also give you sound advice you can use to further your own success. Many of my clients want me to coach them, and as a consequence, they make a lot more progress and have far better outcomes than they would have if they had worked on their own. As you learn more, develop more, and improve, you get better.

"Life will only change when you become more committed to your dreams than you are to your comfort zone." -Billy Cox

Being at a high awareness level means being able to get above fear-based responses and make thoughtful decisions that benefit both you and those around you. There will always be blind spots that we cannot see, no matter how hard we attempt to identify them. When we solicit comments, we can see ourselves from a different viewpoint.

"The comfort zone is the great enemy to creativity; moving beyond it necessitates intuition, which in turn configures new perspectives and conquers fears." -Dan Stevens

You may talk to your friends, family, coworkers, employer, or even acquaintances because they don't have any preconceived notions and can offer unbiased criticism.Establish passive income sources to ensure that your income is unrelated to the amount of time you spend working. Without a doubt, you'll keep working, but only because you want to, not because you have to. Helping others grow is the best way to develop yourself. In the end, there is only one planet. We are all on the same life journey. Either you can focus on the large picture or you may become bogged down in the minute details. The former will enable you to experience life far more fully than the latter.

"I will guarantee you that the day you step outside your comfort zone by making success your goal, is the day you discover that adversity, risk, and daring will make life sweeter than you ever imagined." -Mark Burnett

One day, an old donkey or as fell into a well after slipping. The well was not very deep and had dried up, but the donkey was unable to exit. It started wailing piteously from underneath. The owner and a few people arrived to see the incident. The donkey kept yelling, desperate to escape and terrified for its life. "This foolish donkey will keep shouting," someone said. We can neither use it for work nor sell it because it is already outdated and useless. Anyhow, we wished to plug the well. Now let's get to it. They made the decision to bury the donkey alive after sealing the well. They started filling the well with soil. The donkey would shake off any soil that accidentally landed on its back and stand on top of the mound. The earth continued to rise as it collected. It emerged from the well as soon as they had filled one side of it. The people thought this was a really clever ass. The owner went to the donkey and made an attempt at a hug in thanks. He received a direct kick to the face before fleeing for safety.

"Making the most of any situation that comes your way is a spiritual journey, no matter what someone else tosses at you."

Even though it lacks a brain like yours, a mango tree can transform muck into fruit and sweetness. Plants are able to transform squalor into fragrant blossoms. You ought to be able to transform whatever is presented to you into something lovely. If you can achieve it, it demonstrates who you are. The largest issue on earth is that when little things go wrong, people tend to blame "the little guy" (someone else). They don't appear to be in charge of anything themselves. Stop placing blame or making excuses for other people. Instead, you should strive to reach your full potential.

"The most stupid thing to do is to look outside of yourself for something that only exists within you."

People are gazing skyward in search of happiness and calm. They are searching the entire planet for happiness. It will only occur if you turn inside. We all have our own limitations and comfort zones. Most of us don't frequently leave this since we feel comfortable and secure in our familiar surroundings.The finest professional and personal experiences we may occasionally have, though, come from entirely stepping outside of our comfort zones.We know we attempted something new and probably learnt a lot in the process, even if it was an abysmal failure.

"Whenever you feel uncomfortable, instead of retreating back into your old comfort zone, pat yourself on the back and say, "I must be growing," and continue moving forward." – T. Harv Eker

CHAPTER NINE

Cultivating Happiness Every Day

"It's fine to decide not to decide about something. You just need a decide-not-to-decide system to get it off your mind."
-David Allen

People who are happy plan their acts but not their outcomes.

The goal of human life is to escape the suffering of a material existence and find happiness. Happiness is something we strive for all the time, yet we frequently fall short. Happiness may appear for a moment, but it is fleeting. We cannot avoid suffering, even when we may not desire it. We need to comprehend what is causing our difficulties in the first place so we can fix them. Since the beginning of time, we have been stuck in this material world, and the enjoyment we seek here is fleeting and deceptive.

"Happiness is the art of never holding in your mind the memory of any unpleasant thing that has passed."-Anonymous

We participate in a variety of pious and immoral acts that keep us increasingly tied to this material world in search of such bliss. When we adhere to these three principles, all of the material contamination and sins are washed away, and as a result, we are reinstated in our true constitutional position of limitless pleasure and contentment. Our sorrows are caused by our sinful reactions.

"The moments of happiness we enjoy take us by surprise. It is not that we seize them, but that they seize us."-Ashley Montagu

We cannot avoid suffering, even when we may not desire it. The Vedanta-stra states that we are spiritual beings, an integral part of the Supreme Lord Sri Krishna, and that we are naturally joyful creatures, or nandamayo 'bhyst. So why do we endure pain? How can we find our lost happiness again and live happy lives? Let's first identify the underlying causes of the issues that are ruining our lives. Since the beginning of time, we have been trapped in this material world, and the enjoyment we seek here is fleeting and deceptive. We participate in a variety of pious and immoral acts that keep us increasingly tied to this material world in the pursuit of such happiness. When we adhere to these three principles, all of the material contamination and sins are washed away, and as a result, we are reinstated in our true constitutional position of limitless bliss and contentment.

"Every day, remind yourself that you can choose to be happy. Nobody, nothing, or success can make you happy; nobody else can either." Dr. Amit Das

This is a wonderful illustration of how you might occasionally truly "find" your purpose? When you are exhausted, it is much simpler to sit on the sofa and watch a feel-good programme than it is to go out to dinner with your family, but what good is it to do that? We all squander much too much time on pointless activities. It is preferable to create lasting friendships now. There are also millions of lonely people in the world who would kill to have a dinner companion. maximising life's happiness to the fullest. I have to go home, but I have a choice between taking the five-minute subway ride underground or taking a 30-minute leisurely stroll through a park and through streets lined with trees. Living with purpose produces lasting happiness.

"It isn't what you have, or who you are, or where you are, or what you are doing that makes you happy or unhappy. It is what you think about."-Dale Carnegie

When we are aroused by things we enjoy, this organic chemical is released. These factors induce short-term happiness because they trigger the release of dopamine in response to a single occurrence. The enjoyment will be lost after this event has ended. Consequently, I classify this as short-term happiness. There is also long-term happiness. Since long-term pleasure is based on other ideas of happiness, it is a little more difficult to express. Feeling content with your life's purpose, your accomplishments, your triumphs, and/or your identity and self-worth will help you live a long and happy life. Long-term happiness is founded on ideas that aren't brought about by just one thing.

"We tend to forget that happiness doesn't come as a result of getting something we don't have, but rather of recognizing and appreciating what we do have."-Frederick Keonig

You'll probably feel unsatisfied and dissatisfied if you copy and paste the goals of someone you admire and like.

For instance, Elon Musk, for instance, is accomplishing some amazing things, but if I were in his position, I wouldn't be content. My life's mission is very different from his! I have determined my own life's purpose, and I suggest that you do the same. How do you discover your life's purpose? Therefore, how do you find your purpose?

"In our lives, change is unavoidable, loss is unavoidable. In the adaptability and ease with which we experience change, lies our happiness and freedom."-Buddha

Here's how you can't locate it: by spending the entire day on a chair waiting for it to find you. By repeatedly doing the same things, you will not find your purpose. Instead, you discover it by doing and doing (new) things. It's also critical to understand that your career and your life's mission are not the same. Too many individuals search for a profession that may also fulfil their sense of purpose in life. Only a very tiny number of people truly find meaning in their jobs. To shorten a long story Another illustration of a person who has a meaningful life is I was graciously given the opportunity to hear how another individual I've met leads a meaningful life.

"It's the moments that I stopped just to be, rather than do, that have given me true happiness."-
Richard Branson

One of the most widespread myths about living a meaningful life is that it depends on how much money, power, or position a person has amassed. Even if these "goals" have been accomplished, a void still exists, as if something is missing from their lives. Although everyone is different, living a purposeful life should be based on what their spirit is genuinely yearning for to fill the vacuum. It should not be dependent on what society has prescribed. The capacity and freedom to live your life however you wish to is one of the most magnificent benefits of being a person.

"Others may know pleasure, but pleasure is not happiness. It has no more importance than a shadow following a man."-Muhammad Ali

There isn't a prescriptive law or manual that tells people how to have meaningful lives. It is more of a personal guideline on how to live a happy life. In other words, if you aren't living out your soul's calling and doing the things that make you feel whole and loved by yourself, nothing else really counts. The good news is that there are things you can do to promote and strengthen your feeling of purpose in life. That's accurate. It is possible to live purposefully, to pursue your passions, and to connect your life with your values. Reaching within and seeking a more meaningful existence may seem like a challenging endeavour. Despite the fact that this is far from the case, You may start living with purpose and leading a better, more satisfying life by paying attention to this advice.

"A calm and modest life brings more happiness than the pursuit of success combined with constant restlessness."-Albert Einstein

Everyone aspires to lead a meaningful life. It's a trait of humanity that stems from our dislike of feeling motionless. We must continue to advance toward a target or objective. Without it, we are less content. However, it's simpler said than done. What does living a life with meaning entail? Living with purpose entails pursuing a significant goal that aligns with your beliefs and passions and makes you happy.

"Happiness consists more in small conveniences or pleasures that occur every day, than in great pieces of good fortune that happen but seldom to a man in the course of his life."-Benjamin Franklin

Finding your mission in life is not always simple, so this is more difficult than it seems. This book explains what you can do right away to discover your mission and get started living it. I've included real-world examples of people who have discovered their purpose and lead meaningful lives. How to have a better body image? We all have varied tastes, which is fortunate given that we are all a variety of sizes and forms. If you want to be more body positive, you need to come to this awareness. An estimated 8 million Americans are thought to have an eating disorder of some kind, yet many of them never obtain a formal diagnosis.

"Being happy doesn't mean everything is perfect. It means you've decided to look beyond the imperfections."-
Anonymous

We have a complicated relationship with our bodies. The vehicle in which we travel is our body. The picture that people perceive is what it is. Our bodily image represents us inadvertently. And regrettably, we have little control over how other people see our bodies. The way we perceive ourselves in the mirror and how we think other people view us both influence how we feel about our bodies. This article claims that a person with a good body image is at ease with both their appearance and their feelings. Despite the fact that they are not flawless, they accept themselves. They understand that who they are on the inside matters more than who they are on the outside, and this is maybe what matters most. On the other hand, the same article asserts that a person with a poor body image suffers from profound self-unhappiness. For what purpose? for society? Do you believe that these adjustments will bring happiness? Sometimes all we need to find pleasure is to accept ourselves as we are.

"The happiest people in the world are those who feel absolutely terrific about themselves, and this is the natural outgrowth of accepting total responsibility for every part of their life."-Brian Tracy

Different types of happiness exist. Not just in how we categorise happiness, but also in how we really feel it. It's crucial to understand how these variations might affect the choices we make on a daily basis and whether we live with or without a purpose. Short-term contentment Happiness in the short term is rather simple to describe. It is based on modest, simple means of enjoyment.

"Optimism is a happiness magnet. If you stay positive, good things and good people will be drawn to you."-
Mary Lou Retton

People who are interested in finding actual contentment practise when it isn't convenient, in contrast to others who like talking about having a satisfied life. After all, practise is what gives purpose. We frequently feel the need to multitask while we go about our daily lives. For example, we may watch TV or play with our phones while we eat, engage in discussions while working, or perform home chores or other tasks while on the phone with someone. The reason this is an issue, though, is because nothing is ever completed to our satisfaction, and ultimately, we have only ever performed mediocrely on everything.

"Plenty of people miss their share of happiness, not because they never found it, but because they didn't stop to enjoy it."-William Feather

On the other hand, when we keep our attention on one activity at a time, we complete it entirely before going on to the next one. This not only enables us to perform significantly more admirably, but it also provides us with the chance to experience delight and amazement in even the smallest aspects of our lives. This follows logically from existing in the present moment. We won't ever be distracted by anything other than our current condition if we only ever pay attention to one item. We frequently put off making adjustments. We put off starting a new goal until after the holidays, pick up our workout regimen again after our vacation is over, and often establish timelines for when we will start doing so. But if we put off carrying out the goals we've set for ourselves, we are in essence putting off our purpose.

"If you want to be happy, do not dwell in the past, do not worry about the future, focus on living fully in the present."
— Roy T. Bennett, The Light in the Heart

Why would we wait for something to happen if it is significant enough to us that it will enable us to achieve our goals for being here? Instead, by making adjustments to our lives now rather than later, we will be better able to achieve our goals. Start changing your diet today with your next meal rather than tomorrow's first meal.

"Happiness always looks small while you hold it in your hands, but let it go, and you learn at once how big and precious it is."-Maxim Gorky

Your sadhana is a scientific method for achieving both short-term and long-term wellness. You must purge your thoughts of unneeded clutter if you want your sadhana to be fruitful. You are responsible for cultivating the soil. If you plant a seed on a rock, it won't even start to grow. If you keep accumulating other people's trash, nothing will be able to sprout. Nowadays, most people have too much garbage in their brains to be able to see the enormous potential that is being shown to them. I don't want you to squander your life by being unaware of this option.

"Happiness is something that comes into our lives through doors we don't even remember leaving open."-
Rose Lane

You may be familiar with the tale of Socrates, who was regarded as being very intelligent even during his lifetime. One day, someone approached him and said, "I want to tell you something about Diogenes." "I have a basic principle," Socrates declared. You must pass your speech through the triple filter no matter what you wish to express. What exactly is this triple filter, the guy enquired? First of all, have you verified the truth of whatever it is you are about to tell me now? asked Socrates. "No," the man replied. I was just informed about this. So it doesn't pass the first filter, Socrates remarked. Is it something nice? This is the second filter. No, just the contrary, and that's why I'm telling you. "So it doesn't pass the second filter either," Socrates remarked. Is there any use for it? "No, I don't believe it's beneficial," the guy said. I just wanted to let you know this. "That indicates it doesn't pass any of the filters," Socrates replied. Keep in mind these three filters: Have they made sure that what they wish to tell you is the whole truth before they disclose it to you? Is it a positive trait in someone? Is it beneficial? You will have a lot of mental room to do beneficial, lovely, and spiritual things if you filter out everything that does not fit these three criteria, from what people want to tell you or what you want to tell someone else.

"Happiness is when what you think, what you say, and what you do are in harmony."-
Mahatma Gandhi

You will constantly be occupied with rubbish if you feed yourself unfiltered knowledge, whether it is someone else's or your own. Never enjoy someone else's troubles by spreading rumours about them. You might decide to refrain from criticising someone while you are not speaking to them directly. Spending time mulling over anything someone said or did is a waste of time. Most of you are not in a mental state where, when you close your eyes, you have no more awareness of the outside world. If such is the case, the best course of action is to exhaust yourself completely, leaving no energy for anything that is not essential for your welfare.

"Happiness is not in the mere possession of money; it lies in the joy of achievement, in the thrill of creative effort."-Franklin D. Roosevelt

The alternative to boredom, idleness, resentment, or sorrow is to pass away from weariness. You do not have to decrease your activities because you are getting older. You will only be able to accomplish more if you continue doing something with a great deal of energy and engagement. A young cowherd took his cows into the forest one day to graze. A cow there gave birth to a calf. He saw a birth for the first time. To him, it was a marvel that this tiny fragment of life appeared out of nowhere. He took up the calf and embraced it out of profound love and care for it. And as it was unable to walk, he carried it back home on his shoulders. He carried the calf on his shoulders once more the next day as he took his cows to the forest, and he continued to do so every day.

"When one door of happiness closes, another opens, but often we look so long at the closed door that we do not see the one that has been opened for us."-Helen Keller

The little calf eventually developed into a large bull. The man's strength rose with its weight. All of the residents of the town believed him to be Superman by the time he was seen walking around with a fully grown bull on his shoulders. I want to see those kinds of superpeople everywhere. You shouldn't restrict your abilities. Let's find the boundary that life imposes. Limiting oneself prevents people from making anything significant. It's crucial that you make the most of your life as possible in all respects. Why waste time on things that aren't important when life is so short? Either you must take action to promote your inner well-being or you must help those around you. Whatever sadhana you perform will be far more successful if you fall asleep as soon as your head hits the pillow, since you've used up all of your energy for the day.

"There is only one cause of unhappiness: the false beliefs you have in your head, beliefs so widespread, so commonly held, that it never occurs to you to question them."-Anthony de Mello

Do not waste time mulling over what to do and what to avoid. Your life will become pleasant, and travelling will become simple, if you go from being reluctant to being willing, from being inert to being effervescent. And you'll realise that you led a remarkable life when you look back after you pass away. I consider it very crucial that this occurs for you. Be extraordinary and shine a light on the world. You and I will both burn. There are two methods for dealing with your life. Setting and pursuing goals is one strategy. What sort of objectives will you set? Something about the world that you find impressive, something you haven't done yet, or something that hasn't happened yet in your life. You're making an effort to act or seem like someone else, or to follow their lead. Whatever objectives you choose, they are all somewhat constrained by what you already know, or perhaps just somewhat exaggerated versions of it. Is it not sad to attempt to accomplish something you already know for an entire year? My goal is for things to happen to you that you are unaware of.

"Success is not the key to happiness. Happiness is the key to success. If you love what you are doing, you will be successful."-Herman Cain

Things should come into your life that you never could have anticipated. Your life won't be completely enhanced till then. Why limit yourself to what you already know how to do? Simply state that at the end of the day, you must be a little happier, a little more improved, and a little better than when you made objectives for the entire year. This will not succeed as a goal; it is preferable to consider it in hindsight. Tomorrow evening, just ask yourself, "Am I a bit better than yesterday?" Simply taking a glance at these twenty-four hours can increase your awareness. You're not supposed to feel happy or at ease about this. You should be aware of as many facets of your life as possible.

"We begin from the recognition that all beings cherish happiness and do not want suffering. It then becomes both morally wrong and pragmatically unwise to pursue only one's own happiness oblivious to the feelings and aspirations of all others who surround us as members of the same human family. The wiser course is to think of others when pursuing our own happiness."-Dalai Lama

CHAPTER TEN

Increase Personal Productivity

"Excellence is an art won by training and habituation. We do not act rightly because we have virtue or excellence, but we rather have those because we have acted rightly. We are what we repeatedly do. Excellence, then, is not an act but a habit." -Will Durant

There's always a way to do it better.

Personal productivity is the effective completion of tasks that advance your goals while preserving equilibrium in significant spheres of your life. Depending on what's important to you, being more productive on a personal level may imply many things, such as fostering social connections, improving one's health, or boosting one's income. In the end, setting the proper priorities is the key to achieving your objectives while avoiding burnout.

"Productivity is never an accident. It is always the result of a commitment to excellence, intelligent planning, and focused effort." -Paul J. Meyer

Productivity is not only a trendy word. Personal productivity is the effectiveness with which you continuously execute things that are essential to you. The topic of productivity is frequently brought up in relation to the job. However, given the growing overlap between our personal and professional lives, we should value personal productivity equally.

"Effective performance is preceded by painstaking preparation" -Brian Tracy

When most individuals strive to be more productive, they concentrate on how to get more done in a day rather than considering if those things actually warrant taking up so much time and energy. Put your focus on what you can work on rather than setting a goal that you can compete in a single day. In actuality, little or no management activities are frequently those that may be finished in a single day.

That is to say, they are essential, but they won't significantly advance your life, and more importantly, they shouldn't serve as the yardstick by which you judge your productivity. Because they lack a broad, long-term vision for what their life should be, a lot of people become trapped attempting to complete an increasing number of those little, everyday activities.

"Sometimes, things may not go your way, but the effort should be there every single night." --Michael Jordan

This occurs as a result of people trying to attain goals that are excessively particular rather than constructing their life goals based on values, emotions, and "big picture" elements. You must sit down and write out your ultimate vision for your life as the first and most crucial step towards changing your life and moving ahead.

"People often remark that I'm pretty lucky. Luck is only important in so far as getting the chance to sell yourself at the right moment. After that, you've got to have talent and know how to use it." --Frank Sinatra

Don't forget to think about how you want to feel, what you want to do every day, who you want to be with, and how you want to spend your time. Place a printed copy of it on the wall in front of your primary workspace. Frequently, what's actually not working in our lives isn't what's hurting us the most; rather, it's what makes us feel the least inspired and driven. Pain is a tough thing since it really plays a role in achieving most of our objectives. Not at all. What we're seeking to prevent is suffering and discomfort. However, lack of drive, indifference, and apathy are These are the clear symptoms that you aren't working on a project that actually interests you, and you should reconsider. Use your past blunders as a type of manual for what not to do rather than criticising where you are right now.

"Believe in yourself! Have faith in your abilities! Without a humble but reasonable confidence in your own powers you cannot be successful or happy." --Norman Vincent Peale

Being aware of your dissatisfaction with how a certain course of action affected you is highly important information to have. Appreciate that you were ready to take chances and try new things instead of viewing it as a moral failing or a sign of your lack of value or skill, and go on with even more wisdom about what you do and don't care about, as well as what works and doesn't for your life. One place of one's own is one of the fundamental requirements for humans to flourish. A workstation, a bedroom, a whole apartment, or a house can all qualify as this. The key is to claim some real estate and put some effort into making it a place you not only want to be but also somewhere that motivates you to become the person you really want to be. If your home is full of mementos from the past, ones that don't evoke happy recollections or encourage new ideas, you won't be able to move ahead. If your desk is messy and it bothers you, you won't be able to move forward.

"You were born to win, but to be a winner, you must plan to win, prepare to win, and expect to win." --Zig Ziglar

If you don't actively make the effort to create an area where your work is expressly defined, you will never feel at ease anywhere. It's crucial, yet frequently disregarded. Remember that your frame of reference is limited to what you have experienced when you envision how your life will be in the coming year and beyond. You'll probably feel a little uneasy or frightened when you imagine something that is better than what you have previously experienced.

"No matter how many personal productivity techniques you master, there will always be more to do than you can ever accomplish in the time you have available to you, no matter how much it is." --Brian Tracy

A surprising level of dread is typically also accompanied by significant, broad change. Accept this as it comes. Be receptive to how your life may develop in ways that go beyond what you can now imagine. The reason why most individuals succumb to their worst tendencies isn't because they lack the desire to change their lives drastically; rather, it's that they don't realise that breakthroughs don't just happen on their own. They are an outcome of microshifts.

"Efficiency is doing things right; effectiveness is doing the right things."-Peter Drucker

Let's take the scenario where you wish to slim down. Your body will be shocked if you start changing your food and exercise programme too radically, and you'll rapidly return to your cosy homeostasis. Instead, begin with subtle, nearly imperceptible adjustments. Let's suppose you only eat one snack each day (let's suppose it has a total caloric value of 250). If everything else in your life remained the same, you would lose a pound every two weeks, or 26 pounds in a year. All from skipping a single snack. The purpose isn't to praise dieting methods (most "dieting" doesn't work, anyhow), but rather to emphasise how even seemingly insignificant behaviours may have a significant influence on your life and how altering these habits can affect major aspects of your life. It's often a lot easier than you think.

"The really happy people are those who have broken the chains of procrastination, those who find satisfaction in doing the job at hand. They're full of eagerness, zest, productivity. You can be, too." -- Norman Vincent Peale

If you try to design your life around what you believe will provide you with the most comfort, you will be constantly disappointed. The question is actually what you feel is worth the agony, since nothing in life is without its own unique set of difficulties. A productive year doesn't always imply you finished a lot of unimportant chores. It indicates that you have been intentional with your time and have made efforts to improve your future enjoyment of life. Consider this when you are working each day: Could I do this for the rest of my life? If not, why not? That will provide a wealth of information about what is and isn't actually effective.

"If you are going to achieve excellence in big things, you develop the habit in little matters. Excellence is not an exception, it is a prevailing attitude."-Charles R. Swindoll

Regardless of who you are or what stage of life you are in, organising your funds is essential. Working on lowering your monthly expenses, maintaining a low overhead, paying off debt, and increasing your emergency savings and investment capital will be critical for allowing you to take risks, stabilise your life, and reduce your financial anxiety.

I'm sorry to have to break it to you, but scaling up in your company, lowering your weight by 10 pounds, and improving your profit margin won't make you happy. Such tangible progress is crucial. Not nothing, really. But it's not everything either. Instead of listening to your emotionally charged self-talk story about your life, connect to your reality and start living it.

"The biggest risk is not taking any risk... In a world that changing really quickly, the only strategy that is guaranteed to fail is not taking risks."- Mark Zuckerberg, Facebook

You may experience true joy every day by focusing on the present and all that you have to be thankful for in it. In order to accomplish this, you must ask yourself what is actually occurring as opposed to what is occurring in your internal narrative. Perhaps you've always struggled with money, so you think that one of your main objectives should be to increase your income. In actuality, you could be financially secure and prefer to focus on hobbies or personal interests outside of work. You must keep in mind that frequently, what we desire most is simply what we need.

"Opportunity is missed by most people because it is dressed in overalls and looks like work."-Thomas Edison

Above everything else, we look for familiarity and comfort. Perhaps posting often on social media and working to create a community around your product or service are requirements of your company plan. If so, set aside a day to plan and draught every article, then use a scheduling tool to schedule postings for the following week, month, or longer. Be careful to make it as simple and accessible as possible for yourself to do the things you care about and need to prioritise.

"If you cannot do great things, do small things in a great way." -Napolean Hill

If a coffee shop is where you produce your finest work, go there. Disable your push alerts if you need peace and quiet to concentrate. Make it simple for you to continue to meet your needs. Your energy, not your time, is limited on a daily basis. The major secret is that the direction that the majority of your energy is focused on directly affects your life. If you want to make significant changes, decide what matters most to you and what matters least to you, and then let those things go. If you are unable to locate someone to assist you, consider if you actually require it. Use your energy on something you truly care about if the response is a resounding nay.

"Life is short, live it. Love is rare, grab it. Anger is bad, dump it. Fear is awful, face it. Memories are sweet, cherish them"- Anonymous

If you don't allow yourself to be happy and allow your life to be excellent right here and right now, you may work on your life for the next 12 months straight and, while making a lot of external progress, you won't feel very different on the inside. Nothing short of altering your daily thoughts and emotions will alter your outlook, perspective, or internal narrative that governs your thoughts and feelings. I'll start now. Not until you've made more progress. Not once you've changed or improved. In reality, altering your life only entails altering your current state of being. The rest will be handled automatically.

"Plans are nothing; planning is everything." --Dwight D. Eisenhower

Instant gratification is alluring and enjoyable, but it shouldn't come at the price of long-term objectives, particularly those that will help you improve your self-esteem and move you closer to your objectives. You will undoubtedly come across an explanation or justification if you are seeking one not to act morally. Unless you did anything to deserve a response, the likelihood is that when someone makes a comment, offers unsolicited advice, or treats you rudely, the statement says more about the person than it does about you.

"Walk away from anything or anyone who takes away from your joy. Life is too short to put up with fools"-
Anonymous

Change into some new clothing and go workout if you need to feel better right now. Endorphins make you joyful, relieve tension, and aid in mental clarity. Get some perspective by working out first, then returning to the subject. It's likely that after exercising, your emotions will be more stable, your intellect will be sharper, and your anxiety level will be lower than before.

"There are risks and costs to action. But they are far less than the long-range risks of comfortable inaction."
--John F. Kennedy

Therefore, try to see if you can get some exercise before you make a choice if you panic and feel overwhelmed by whatever you have been faced with. You'll come to a judgement that is less emotional and more based on logic than on emotion. Start attempting to track and modify these behaviours if you see that you spend a lot of time looking at multiple devices, frequently checking social media, or aimlessly using your phone. Whatever your primary source of ineffectiveness is, learn to control it so you can become more efficient and stop wasting time.

"He who asks is a fool for five minutes, but he who does not ask remains a fool forever."-Anonymous

You do have some influence over your life at any given time; you are not a victim of every whim and situation. Whether you can alter your circumstances depends on how you use that control. The sooner you stop avoiding taking responsibility for your life and stop blaming others, the more autonomy you will have, the sooner you will start doing the work, and the sooner you will start progressing.

"I feel that luck is preparation meeting opportunity."-Oprah Winfrey

Living your life selfishly for yourself will not bring you the most fulfilment. The times when we are choosing to contribute to others are when we experience the most happiness and fulfilment, on the other hand. Every day, give someone else your life. Encourage a young person. Support a coworker. Support a nearby nonprofit. Or simply give your friend who needs to hear from you a call. You have aspirations, objectives, and hopes in addition to the daily needs of existence.

"Paying attention to the minor things rather than the big ones is the foundation of success in life."- Booker T. Washington

You enjoy doing hobbies and participating in activities that define who you are. Take use of these possibilities to live. And each day, engage in one activity you enjoy. We all have tasks that we need to complete, including projects, jobs, and obligations. Most likely, you can't complete everything on your to-do list in a single day. But to get the most out of today, choose one major item off your list and complete it first. If you're done, go to the next one. Our days are made up primarily of single days that follow one another. The sun rises, sets, and rises once more. And ultimately, the lives we decide to lead will depend on the way we choose to live each day.

"It is not enough to be busy, so are the ants. The question is: What are we busy about?" – Henry David Thoreau

It won't be easy to increase your personal productivity, but every obstacle you overcome is a chance to get better. Since people have been trying to increase productivity ever since the dawn of time, it's not surprising that there are so many quotations on the subject. The fact that "productivity" applies to practically every facet of life doesn't help. You will learn to better manage your time, energy, and attention by learning from the distractions you encounter and the errors you make. The simple fact that you have a North Star will inspire you to keep moving forward despite all of the potential barriers.

"Use your mind to think about things, rather than think of them. You want to be adding value as you think about projects and people, not simply reminding yourself they exist."

- David Allen

CHAPTER ELEVEN

Make Value-Based Decisions

"Values are like fingerprints. Nobodies are the same but you leave them all over everything you do."-Elvis Presley

Your moral compass define who you are.

In a world full of uncertainty, no one can guarantee tomorrow. I wanted my readers or students to have a set of guiding principles because I was inspired by the birth of my children. I wanted children to be aware of our family's values at all times. In this age of growing connectivity and technology, fewer and fewer individuals have their own moral compass. There is a constant barrage of media that aims to grab our attention and instil terror in our thoughts. This book is not restricted to parents of young children. All families or people who want to create their own legacy should do this. You may start by setting a purpose, making the required preparations, and writing down your rules for living.

"Peace of mind produces right values, right values produce right thoughts. Right thoughts produce right actions."-Mark Richardson

A moral compass is a clear feeling of integrity and the will to act morally. When making decisions in life, everyone of us is influenced by our moral compass and conscience. Your character will constantly be strengthened by doing this, making you a person of great worth and ideals. There are certain people, nevertheless, who lack this moral compass and engage in unethical behaviour. But you should always possess the guts to act morally. You will always find success and peace of mind if your moral compass and conscience are clear in all aspects of your life—personal, professional, and workplace.

"The biggest challenge, I think, is always maintaining your moral compass." -Barack Obama

After reading this book, take the first step if you want to start anything new. Start right away to avoid missing out on your chance to achieve your goals. When we're not paying attention to the here and now, what are we thinking about? Either we are lamenting the past or we are fearing the future. Can we exert influence over something that hasn't even happened yet? Naturally, because the answer to both of those questions is "no," the only thing left to worry about is the present.

"When values, thoughts, feelings, and actions are in alignment, a person becomes focused and character is strengthened."-John C. Maxwell

How to improve your life? Are you ready to improve yourself? No Comparative Because of social media, we've developed a strong habit of contrasting our lives with those of others. Everyone else's life seems so perfect; why can't mine? Self-talk like this needs to cease. You need to quit worrying so much about what other people are doing and start concentrating on your own particular ambitions if you want to truly enjoy life.

"I have learned that as long as I hold fast to my beliefs and values, and follow my own moral compass, then the only expectations I need to live up to are my own."
-Michelle Obama

Being selfish once in a while is not harmful. Take a break from the screen and spend some "me time." Being Present Because it's so crucial, people frequently say to "live in the moment." The amazing things that are taking place right now are being overlooked because we are either too preoccupied with remembering the past or planning the future. When you squander time wishing it away or daydreaming about events that happened in the past, time goes by very quickly. Try to focus as much of your attention as you can on being in the present moment. Yoga is the ideal way to begin to practise mindfulness.

"Good values are like a magnet – they attract good people."-John Wooden

Show your appreciation In order to truly maximise your life, self-reflection is essential. Sometimes it's necessary to remind ourselves of all the great things we have to be thankful for since we often focus more on what we don't have than what we do. Maybe you have a terrific group of friends or a job you enjoy. Make an effort to reflect. If necessary, start a gratitude journal and write down three things each day for which you are grateful. It's a great tool for perspective-setting since it may make what seemed like a terrible day not so horrible after all.

"Your core values are the deeply held beliefs that authentically describe your soul."-John C. Maxwell

We understand that you're busy, hungry, and sleepy. But doing as much exercise as you can each day can improve your mood significantly. It not only encourages greater health, but it also makes you stronger and more fit for upcoming excursions. The hardest thing is getting started; after you've done that, the muscle-toning endorphin surges continue nonstop.

"Define your priorities, know your values and believe in your purpose. Only then can you effectively share yourself with others."-Les Brown

We do our best to remain in our growth zone, though. That mysterious space between our comfort zone and our panic zone is our growth zone. It's where we develop as people, and it doesn't just involve getting better at what we're doing; it also teaches us courage and self-assurance when we discover that we can perform tasks successfully even when we don't feel entirely at ease or confident doing them. Because being confident doesn't mean you're free of anxiety, tension, or any other negative emotion.

"Live your days on the positive side of life, in tune with your most treasured values. And in each moment you'll have much to live for."-Ralph Marston

Confident means knowing that you can carry out your obligations despite the presence of those emotions. Though somewhat less frequently than others, these emotions are nonetheless felt by the most self-assured individuals. And when they do, they make sure that those feelings don't keep them back by employing the same techniques that you're about to discover.

"Values reflect what is important to the way you live and work."- Anonymous

You can only truly possess confidence if you realise that anxiety or tension won't prevent you from carrying out your goals and duties, any more than a slight morning hangover will prevent you from attending work or school. Maintain your whole commitment to the idea and continue to nourish and fertilise it through activities as and when the mood strikes. This will prevent possible blockages from occurring by keeping you in your flow rather than placing you under excessive pressure.

"Achievement of your happiness is the only moral purpose of your life, and that happiness, not pain or mindless self-indulgence, is the proof of your moral integrity, since it is the proof and the result of your loyalty to the achievement of your values."-Ayn Rand

We need to understand the distinction between stressful and traumatic experiences in order to determine what is in our growth zone. Because stress is not only beneficial when attempting to grow, it is also required. I suppose trauma should be avoided. Again, when I refer to trauma, I mean anything that makes us want to hide away, run away, vomit, or cry. This is your reflex to fight, flee, or freeze. Typically, you will either feel extremely irritated and angry, physically flee the situation, or utterly freeze and lose all ability to think, act, or speak. You are in your panic zone at this point. If it does, go back and reconsider what you had planned to do.

"Apart from values and ethics which I have tried to live by, the legacy I would like to leave behind is a very simple one - that I have always stood up for what I consider to be the right thing, and I have tried to be as fair and equitable as I could be."- Ratan Tata

Do you ever feel like you should have accomplished more in life? You can have the overpowering impression that, from where you are right now, you will never get to your objective. Please allow me to allay your concerns. As long as you decide to move forward resolutely, you are in a good position to take any course. When you lose touch with your authentic self, tension develops. An inner voice that won't be pleased until it gets what it wants only serves to exacerbate this. I refer to it as the inner critic, which rules your mental process and is ingrained from an early age.

"If we are to go forward, we must go back and rediscover those precious values - that all reality hinges on moral foundations and that all reality has spiritual control."-Martin Luther King, Jr.

No matter how fulfilling you think your life is, there's always somewhere else you want to be. You never feel content because your ego always tells you to chase your next goal in order to find happiness. Do you have that feeling? Is it true that you are sad and want something better—a better relationship, a better financial situation, a better job, or more material possessions? However, when they do, you are only momentarily content. The thrill soon wears off, and you go out in search of the next adventure to keep you engrossed.

I compare it to the scurrying white rabbit from the Alice in Wonderland story, who keeps checking his pocket watch and saying, "Oh dear! I'm sorry! I'll arrive too late! Moving from one place to another without stopping to recognise your accomplishments gives you that impression. Instead of living your life, you're eluding it by avoiding seeing reality as it is.

"Just as your car runs more smoothly and requires less energy to go faster and farther when the wheels are in perfect alignment, you perform better when your thoughts, feelings, emotions, goals, and values are in balance."- Brian Tracy

Because you naively follow a goal without understanding the motivations behind it, this results in a barren existence.It appears as though you are attempting to control the future as you envision it. Everyone is aware that life rarely goes as expected. Your well-crafted plans will inevitably be derailed by diversions and roadblocks.

"Set out your daily activities so that time works for you rather than against you."

If you go from one goal to another without applying what you've learned, you miss out on important life lessons. Years later, you regret the fantastic possibilities that you missed while living your best life. Everyone has a unique calling or purpose in life, and each person is tasked with completing a certain task. Because of this, neither his life nor his replacement are possible. As a result, each person's work and the opportunity to complete it are distinct. To be present to what is happening, it is necessary to perceive life in the context of the larger picture.

"Wherever I go meeting the public... spreading a message of human values, spreading a message of harmony, is the most important thing."- Dalai Lama

You miss out on the essential lessons woven into your trip if you categorise every encounter as good or negative. Life is a series of gifts, but only if you choose to use them. Starting where you are means appreciating your existing situation. To live a life with meaning, you don't need to have all the knowledge, money, or ideal circumstances. What is needed is a dedication to making baby steps ahead while trusting that the road will become clear as long as you have a clear intention.

According to research by United Healthcare, 93% of volunteers reported feeling happy as a consequence. Additionally, 88% reported higher self-esteem. 85% of people who volunteered made new acquaintances. 79% had less stress. Make an action plan for your objectives and put them into action! It has a list of things to complete before passing away. Then set out to accomplish them. Always consider your actions, and only carry them out if they have a purpose.

"Our morality is based on so many factors: of where we were born, who we were born to, what values were instilled in us, what values we chose, the way that our lives have shaped us. That dictates so much of what we assume is our morality, and also the culture, all of these things."- Oscar Isaac

Our thoughts shut off as a result of boredom and restlessness, and we become more docile. Let's not deceive ourselves; neither your history nor your future are shaped by it, any more than the weather last week predicts the weather five years from now. Given your degree of knowledge, your history has brought you to this location in time. Because you prioritise personal development, you are reading this, which is an indication of advancement. There will definitely be diversions, setbacks, difficulties, and failures along your life's road.

"It was character that got us out of bed, commitment that moved us into action, and discipline that enabled us to follow through."- Zig Ziglar

Other than the certainty that you can realise your full potential, nothing is definite. Regardless of what we experience, living with purpose can help us be more resilient and perhaps even grow. Because they struggle with false ideas about how life should be, the majority of individuals play the game of life while pinned to the ropes. This is a surefire prescription for failure since your ideas about life don't actually make it happen; instead, they only generate agony and unhappiness.

"The right moral compass is trying hard to think about what customers want."-Sundar Pichai

Instead, I'm content because I was able to put a lot of effort into things that gave me a sense of purpose and because I was able to accomplish things that made me extremely proud. As a result, without depending on specific occurrences, I have established a condition in which I am content by default. I believe that my intentional way of living has contributed to some of this. A happy life is one that has a purpose.

"The men can have a moral compass that is just unshakeable, they can have ethics that run to the core."
-Lupe Fiasco

You have considerably more influence over your long-term satisfaction when you live your life with a purpose. You won't feel like you're working toward some nebulous objective that doesn't make you happy while merely floating along. Your long-term enjoyment, fulfilment, and sense of accomplishment are much easier to define when you have a purpose. You can guide your life in the most beneficial way when you have a purpose. And it is along that path that you may find lasting happiness!

"Real integrity is doing the right thing, knowing that nobody's going to know whether you did it or not." -Oprah Winfrey

Many of us unconsciously use social media to divert our attention when we're feeling bad. Perhaps you were hoping I'd suggest you shouldn't do this at all. However, research has indicated a highly variable impact of social media use on wellbeing. Some claim it enhances wellbeing, while others claim the reverse. One piece of research in particular provides a plausible explanation: how you feel about social media is more important than how you use it.

"If people use common sense and their own guiding moral compass, I think they'll generally stay out of trouble."-Steve Chabot

Utilizing the network increases your sense of wellbeing and self-worth if you feel an emotional connection to it and it is a part of your everyday life. Therefore, it probably won't assist you if you're logging in for the first time in a month and you can't even remember who you're linked to. However, there isn't really anything wrong with using it to make you feel like a member of a community.

Never be hesitant to stop doing things that aren't helping you on your journey. It would be a waste of life to do anything else. Don't do anything if you don't enjoy it. Spend your time and effort on activities that make you happy and fulfilled.

What makes you so angry? Find what you enjoy doing by getting out there. Stop doing a job that you find uninteresting. When you're prepared to work it full-time, quit your job. Make your passion into a successful multimillion-dollar enterprise. Make it worth several billions of dollars and even better. Be receptive to criticism but avoid letting it impact you. The goal of criticism is to make you a better person. The glass is either half full or half empty. Why not claim that it is neither?

"The highest possible stage in moral culture is when we recognize that we ought to control our thoughts." -Charles Darwin

Actually, it is completely full; the upper half is air and the bottom half is water. Everything is a question of perspective. Adopt perspectives that will help you, not ones that will limit you. You'll be able to live a life that is significantly richer than others if you can always find the bright side of things. If there is something about someone you dislike, tell him or her directly; if not, keep your mouth shut. Speaking ill of others is rude and shows limited thinking. We will always be narrow-minded and exclusive if everyone simply considers their own point of view. Consider the viewpoints of others.

"The moral compass was only ever a means to an end and the end is survival of the individuals who use it most creatively."- Derek Robertson

Be courteous and compassionate to everyone you come into contact with. Have confidence in your skills and abilities. Replace your limiting thoughts with empowering ones by identifying your limiting beliefs and changing them. How can you expect others to believe in you if you don't believe in yourself? Give those who have harmed you in the past your forgiveness. This includes individuals who have betrayed you, claimed credit for your accomplishments, and harmed you. Don't become obsessed with acquiring a specific position, fame, fortune, or material goods. These are ephemeral and will eventually vanish when you pass away. Instead, concentrate on developing and fully experiencing life. Relationships that don't benefit you should be ended. That includes unfavourable characters, liars, disrespectful individuals, harsh critics, and connections that limit your capacity for development. Spend time with those you get along with, including those who share your interests and who are upbeat, successful, and supportive of your advancement.

"Moral authority comes from following universal and timeless principles like honesty, integrity, treating people with respect." -Stephen Covey

"We spend money we don't have on goods we don't need in an effort to impress unconcerned individuals," William Smith observed. Nobody is impressed by your wealth, stylish attire, or taste in house furnishings. It must be so incredibly tiring to wear all these masks depending on your circumstances at any one time. Why do you think it's necessary for you to put on such a show? Don't let anyone convince you otherwise; you are wonderful just the way you are. Without a shred of guilt, share your original ideas, opinions, peculiarities, and personality traits with the world. Before making a choice, educate yourself and weigh your alternatives, but avoid being mired in uncertainty forever.

"In the worst of times the best among us never lose their moral compass, and that is how they emerge relatively unscathed." - Henry Rollins

Acquire the ability to see each occurrence impartially. So that you can apply the lessons going forward, concentrate on what you can learn from them. Arm yourself with as much knowledge as possible. Learn new things, take up new hobbies, and pursue new subjects of study. Develop a vast breadth of information for yourself. In video games, you can typically only level up to level 99, but in real life, you can level up indefinitely. What would you typically avoid doing? You become aware of who you are and what is significant in your life as you learn to embrace who you are. Perhaps most significantly, you begin to embrace life and truly love being alive.

Nobody will ever stop pointing out the myriad reasons you'll fail or what you're doing incorrectly with each step you take, no matter what you choose to pursue in your life. Recognise that not every loser wins, but every winner suffers. People who become successful don't always succeed. Their perseverance in the face of setbacks is what ultimately makes them successful. To increase your self-confidence and make it impermeable to the outside forces attempting to undermine it, concentrate on setting boundaries and engaging in self-love the next time you encounter a hater. Don't do something if it doesn't seem right. You won't feel satisfied or free from remorse if you compromise your personal code of ethics.

Establish what you value most. The principles that guide your identity and way of life are known as your core values. They could be firmly held spiritual beliefs or just beliefs that are significant to you. You may make "value-congruent" objectives for yourself by reflecting on your values.

"Keep your thoughts positive because your thoughts become your words. Keep your words positive because your words become your behavior. Keep your behavior positive because your behavior becomes your habits. Keep your habits positive because your habits become your values. Keep your values positive because your values become your destiny."-Mahatma Gandhi

CHAPTER TWELVE

Live Life To The Fullest

"We must believe that we are gifted for something and that this thing must be attained. Nothing in life is to be feared; it is only to be understood. I am one of those who thinks, like Nobel, that humanity will draw more good than evil from new discoveries. "
--Marie Curie

If you follow your passion, you can build a life you're proud of.

In his lifetime, Steve Jobs made a lot of progress. When he made those remarks, he argued, "Why else would we be here?" Unless not to act, alter, or accomplish something? To put it another way, our goal is to make a dent in the universe. Indeed, Steve Jobs left his imprint. Even after he has passed away, we still discuss him. Pharaoh Khufu also did so. He left us the great pyramid, though I don't like to credit individuals for a project's success when it's obvious that a group of people worked on it.

You build the meaning of your life every day through the choices you make and the ideas you think. Always consider what you can learn and how you may advance, and refrain from blaming others when things aren't going your way. It's up to you to define what it means to live life to the "fullest."

Life might be dangerous at times, but every benefit comes with some level of risk. You won't advance in life if you never take chances, and you definitely won't discover how to live life to the fullest. The quickest way to get dissatisfied is to stay in your comfort zone. You won't learn anything new, and your personal and professional lives will become stagnant if you don't venture outside of what you're currently comfortable with. Even though it can seem awkward, taking a chance might be as easy as agreeing to go out with your friends the next time they ask rather than remaining home by yourself. It can entail booking a flight to a different place, going on a blind date, or digging up old paintings that have been stashed away for a long time. Find something new to attempt today, and establish objectives that go beyond what you now think is feasible. When individuals reflect on their lives, they regret the risks they didn't take more than the ones they did, so try something new today.

"Carve your name on hearts, not tombstones. A legacy is etched into the minds of others and the stories they share about you."-Shannon Adler

You are unlikely to experience true success or happiness if you believe, as do many people today, that happiness must wait while you succeed and that the ultimate goal of achievement is to abandon all efforts and live a happy life. A hot fudge sundae tastes great on the first bite, but after four, the pleasure is diminished, according to all scientific study on happiness. Instead than searching for some kind of eternal state of bliss, you need to refresh happiness on a regular basis.

For a variety of reasons, having the appropriate mentality is crucial. Not least of all, in your situation, telling yourself that you couldn't do it because you felt so far outside of your comfort zone went against coaching theory and your own principles. You were really conflicted, and this is when your ego, posing as your impostor, sprung into action. Recall what a legacy is and that others who are ready and will benefit from it will see, cherish, and share it. Even if it can sound a little pompous to think about leaving a legacy, we all leave legacies as we live our lives. From the reflection that follows a discussion to the larger legacy a loved one leaves when they pass away to the legacy we leave when we part ways with a customer, team, or job.

Accept yourself as you are. All too frequently, we focus a lot of our attention on the aspects of ourselves that we wish we could alter or that we believe ought to be done differently. You can't concentrate on the future if all of your attention is on what you dislike or what happened in the past. Make the choice to accept and adore yourself just as you are. Be open to flexibility. We anticipate things to remain the same, which is one of the reasons we get dissatisfied. However, change is a constant in life. Learn to adapt to the new circumstances and difficulties that arise by opening yourself up to the processes of change and growth.

"Measuring life by one yardstick won't work. And moving through the four sequentially is a mistake too."-
Warren Buffett

Life is a precious commodity. But how can you maximise your life? Here are some insightful suggestions on how to maximise your time on earth.

- Being present and in the moment is the first step. I really enjoy the little things in life, such as the way flannel blankets feel against your skin, the warmth of a hug, or the gift of a smile. and appreciation.

- Create a magnificently chaotic patchwork of what is real for you and your position in our earthly community by taking all of your activities, beliefs, work, ideas, feelings, and contributions. With laughter and contemplation, they sew the patchwork together.

- Decorate courageously and with love. Recognize that patches occasionally wear out or rip, forcing you to determine whether you can repair them or whether you need to replace them. Pursue your hobbies and dreams right now!

- Never stop learning; develop the capacity for unconditional love and a passion for empirical learning. If certain things take you a while to learn or if you run across obstacles, try not to become upset. This is a necessary component of life.

- Be sincere with others and with yourself. Energy and happiness are drained away by dishonesty. Being dishonest with ourselves prevents us from improving and learning. When we lie to somebody, we erode their trust and connection.

- Accept yourself as you are. All too frequently, we focus a lot of our attention on the aspects of ourselves that we wish we could alter or that we believe ought to be done differently. You can't concentrate on the future if all of your attention is on what you dislike or what happened in the past. Make the choice to accept and adore yourself just as you are.

- Be open to flexibility. We anticipate things to remain the same, which is one of the reasons we get dissatisfied.

However, change is a constant in life. Learn to adapt to the new circumstances and difficulties that arise by opening yourself up to the processes of change and growth.

- Life is not a motion picture. There are many ambiguous places. Do anything you want as long as you can face yourself in the mirror with admiration and affection. Trust your intuition.

- Live each day as though it were your last. Take risks and chances so that when you look back on your life, you can say you lived it to the fullest.

- Look after your body. Every element of your life is impacted by your level of health and fitness. Create and implement a time management strategy.

- The most significant sources of enjoyment in your life will be your connections with close relatives and friends. But you need to exercise caution. You will be persuaded to believe that you may put your investments in these relationships on hold when things at home appear to be going well. That would be a grave error.

- When severe issues in those relationships occur, it's frequently too late to fix them. This means that, almost paradoxically, it is most crucial to invest in creating strong families and personal friendships during times when it would seem unnecessary on the surface.

- Being open to and picky about ideas is one way to maximise your life. More concepts will be encountered, entertained, and pursued as though they were lovely to experience as our language is expanded.

- Stay in the present and show yourself and others love, kindness, and compassion. Evaluate your skills and talents realistically, then search for possibilities to use them in ways that advance human society in the future.

- "Push yourself on occasion." You could have more options than you think. When in doubt, use that other great human strength: the option that shows the most compassion.

- Take care of the ill, injured, and handicapped. Love, love, love, and when you think you have no more to give, love some more! Use your special abilities, knowledge, and insights to benefit others.

- The secret is to identify what makes you happy and useful. Speak up on behalf of those who can't. Make a difference in the life of someone else.

- Take care of your physical and mental health. Help others. and love unconditionally. Be concerned about the well-being of your family.

- Heal yourself if you need to, forgive others if you need to, and learn to love if that is your lesson. To get to the essence of existence, strive for a better, more meaningful life.

- As the answers to who you are and what you are destined to accomplish are personal to each of us, listen, breathe, and look for them. To act despite fear and to acknowledge and accept suffering and hurt.

- Accept and live as our authentic selves. Rely on your own sense of self to view people objectively, to perceive them clearly, and with compassion.

- Always be mindful of the beauty that is there in every moment, no matter how tiny. Give it some serious thought and take some time to properly look.

- Acceptance of being vulnerable You take chances when you live life to the fullest. You pursue your goals. You make choices that have an impact. And occasionally, these things don't turn out as you had intended.

- To live fully, openly, and honestly, we must embrace our vulnerability and the potential that things will not turn out as planned. Contrary to popular belief, people can "catch" emotions just as easily as they can catch colds.
- You're more likely to feel cheerful and optimistic if you spend a lot of time with pleasant and upbeat people. Spending a lot of time among people who only think negatively will make you do the same. Embrace those that appreciate and care for you. Respect you and others. Enrich your life.
- Remain in the present and be certain that we are where we should be. Discover the fundamental nature of the mind by realising that thoughts and emotions are only fleeting clouds in the sky.
- Give someone helpful guidance or wisdom to assist them on their journey. It may significantly alter things. Try to be as present as possible at all times. Stop being so hard on yourself.
- Identify your importance to mankind and the existence of the planet on which we live. Show more consideration, kindness, and gentleness to our planet.We owe it to the environment, the wildlife, our forests, and our seas to bring them back to their former state of health.
- Assemble the things and people that bring you joy. Discover the advantages of knowing and accepting people from all walks of life. Follow your dreams, love the people you care about, and cultivate your spirit.
- Taking in life. Just do it. Don't live an unloved life. Constantly strive to put others' needs ahead of your own. Good karma may be created by doing something as simple as opening a door for someone else, allowing someone to go ahead of you in a line, or saying good

morning to someone who is alone. Volunteer your time.

- Be mindful of your kinship. They are the ones who truly count. Ignore what people think about the way you spend your life. By lowering your expectations, you may simplify your life and take full advantage of it.

- Always strive for love, both giving and receiving it. If you can look back on your life and say that you helped someone else feel loved, then your life was successful.

- Through your actions, words, music, and those you surround yourself with, you may cultivate a calm environment. These are stimulating and can result in fantastic experiences. The mindful abilities of attention, compassion, and acceptance may assist you in transforming unhealthful behaviours into a way of being that symbolises freedom and inner peace.

- Remember to enjoy yourself. Work as hard as you can, and then watch a movie. When you're feeling perplexed, gaze up at the sky and take in how expansive everything is.

- Mindfulness gives a dependable and trustworthy road home. As you become more aware of your body, you will understand how your ideas and the corresponding emotions affect your physiology. Your body will then send signals to your brain about how well you are thinking.

- Make plans and set goals, but be adaptable and resilient if they don't pan out. Peace can exist without you having to free yourself from negative ideas. Instead, turn your attention away from them and onto concepts that will enrich your life.

- Destructive thoughts fade away as you shift your focus to more constructive ideas. You will become a living embodiment of serenity if you do this regularly. Under the garb of a spiritual guru, finding peace is a choice rather than something that calls for intense study.

- Create sincere, real relationships with everyone you come into contact with, including your friends, family, coworkers, business partners, customers, clients, and acquaintances. Spend some time getting to know them better to build a deeper relationship.
- We are given opportunities to practise every day. We give our craft life when we practise it every day as a way of life rather than just a job. It might be a combination of physical, mental, and spiritual exercises.
- You'll know you've started a chain of goodwill because one act of kindness almost always leads to another, which should give you comfort even on the worst of days.
- Recognise what you've learnt from your mistakes, acknowledge that you can't undo the past, and begin to be nicer to yourself. The primary victim of holding a grudge against someone is you.
- The advantages of meditation for the mind-body connection are covered in prior works of mine. Many people think that in order to experience the benefits of this practise, they must spend hours in a contemplative position. We may become mired in misery and disgust with our appearance. Alternately, we might accept who we are and disregard what people say about us.
- As we age, our learning frequently becomes stagnant. However, it's in our nature to always seek out new knowledge and information because otherwise we become bored. Therefore, invest in a book on a subject you are interested in. Enroll in an evening course or a course online.Expanding your knowledge will make you feel amazing, whether it's all theoretical or you're

learning something useful.

"There is no strength where there is no battle."-Oprah Winfrey

When all we experience in life are rainbows, adorable puppies, sugar drops, and sunlight, we have little reason to strive for personal improvement. Don't worry about what others are doing. A crucial component in the quest for success is overlooked when people get wrapped up in the manual that other people use. It does not always follow that something will work for you just because it did for someone else. Every fibre of your being should believe that you are capable of achieving everything you set your mind to.

Life is not a motion picture. There are many ambiguous places. Do anything you want as long as you can face yourself in the mirror with admiration and affection. Trust your intuition. Understanding that life is a journey rather than a destination Life is about how you get where you're going as much as where you go, despite the cliché that goes along with it. It will take you your entire life to learn how to live life to the fullest. If certain things take you a while to learn or if you run across obstacles, try not to become upset. This is a necessary component of life. Be sincere with others and with yourself. Energy and happiness are drained away by dishonesty. Being dishonest with ourselves prevents us from improving and learning. When we lie to somebody, we erode their trust and connection.

"Conformity is the adversary of progress and the prisoner of freedom." -Kennedy, John F

Our profession determines how we live and why we are here. We may have many interests and be many things to many people, but we only devote our entire, daily attention to the skill to which we are devoted. Our resolve to pursue progress every day eventually determines the difference between a life of fulfilment and one of discontentment. We surpass the constraints imposed by our body or psyche.

"Take up one idea. Make that one idea your life; dream of it; think of it; live on that idea. Let the brain, the body, muscles, nerves, every part of your body be full of that idea, and just leave every other idea alone. This is the way to success, and this is the way great spiritual giants are produced."- Swami Vivekanand

References

- *Finding Purpose Beyond Oneself: How to Live a Fulfilling Life & Find Your Life's Work by Focusing on Others Instead of Yourself (15 Minute Life Series Book 1) Kindle Edition by Sean Bobby Maximilian, Nov, 2016.*
- *Finding Your Purpose: How to Find Your Purpose In Life and Make the Most of Your Time Here on Earth, a Non-Religious Perspective - (What is the Purpose of Life ?) Kindle Edition by Kathleen Rao, June, 2014.*
- *Finding Your Passionate Purpose: In Life, Leadership, and Love, November, 2016 by Heidi McKee.*
- *Finding Your WHY: Discover Your Life's Purpose, February, 2015 by Mike Rodriguez.*
- *Know What You Want: The Simple Step-By-Step Guide to Finding Your Passion And Living On Purpose Kindle Edition by Pearce Lee, Aug, 2015.*
- *Discovering Your Personal Potential: Finding God's Will and Purpose for Your Life, December, 2007 by Tobenna O Ebubechukwu.*
- *Man's Search for Meaning Paperback – May, 2006 by Viktor E. Frankl.*
- *Build Your Legacy: 18 Principles To Help You Create And Maintain A Lasting Legacy Paperback – December, 2020 by Chris Flores, Luisa Korpi.*
- *How to Achieve Immortality: 100 Ways to Create Your Own Legacy for Future Generations by Llyod Silverman, Nov,2004.*
- *The Element: How Finding Your Passion Changes Everything, December, 2009 by Ken Robinson , Lou Aron.*
- *12 Rules For Life, January, 2018 by Jordan B. Peterson.*

- *The Untethered Soul: The Journey Beyond Yourself, Oct , 2007 by Michael A. Singer.*
- *Find Your Passion: 25 Questions You Must Ask Yourself, Oct , 2013 by Henri Junttila.*
- *Do the Work: Overcome Resistance and Get Out of Your Own Way, March, 2015 by Steven Pressfield.*
- *Miracles Now: 108 Life-Changing Tools for Less Stress, More Flow, and Finding Your True Purpose, April , 2015 by Gabrielle Bernstein.*
- *The Crossroads of Should and Must: Find and Follow Your Passion, April , 2015 by Elle Luna.*
- *The Happiness of Pursuit: Finding the Quest That Will Bring Purpose to Your Life , April , 2016 by Chris Guillebeau.*
- *Unwrapping Your Passion: Creating the Life You Truly Want, July, 2017 by Karen Putz*
- *The Life You Were Born to Live (Revised 25th Anniversary Edition): A Guide to Finding Your Life Purpose, August , 2018 by Dan Millman.*
- *I Could Do Anything If I Only Knew What It Was: How to Discover What You Really Want and How to Get It, August , 1995 by Barbara Sher.*
- *The Art of Work: A Proven Path to Discovering What You Were Meant to Do, March , 2015 by Jeff Goins.*
- *The Gifts of Imperfection: Let Go of Who You Think You're Supposed to Be and Embrace Who You Are, October, 2010 by Brené Brown.*
- *How to Achieve Immortality: 100 Ways to Create Your Own Legacy for Future Generations Paperback – November, 2004 by Lloyd Silverman.*
- *Make Your Own Luck: How to Increase Your Odds of Success in Sales, Startups, Corporate Career and Life Paperback –October, 2019 by Bob Miglani & Rehan Yar*

Khan.

- *What Is Your Legacy?: 101 Ideas On Getting Started to Create and Build One Kindle Edition by Anca Iovita, July 2021.*
- *Your Legacy In A Book: How to Create a Memoir Your Family Will Cherish For Generations Kindle Edition, February,2022 by Travis Cody.*
- *9 Tips To Take Your Life Back - Simple and helpful tips on organizing your life, melting the stress away, and living a more happier, healthier, & purposeful (Simple Ways To A Stress Free Life Book 1) Kindle Edition, July,2016 by Rich A. Williams.*
- *Finding Purpose Beyond Oneself: How to Live a Fulfilling Life & Find Your Life's Work by Focusing on Others Instead of Yourself (15 Minute Life Series Book 1) Kindle Edition, November,2016 by Sean Bobby Maximilian.*
- *Living A Life Of Purpose: A 10 week study focusing on ways to live a purposeful life Kindle Edition, October,2021 by Marni Ausenbaugh devotional.*
- *Good Vibes, Good Life: How Self-love Is the Key to Unlocking Your Greatness Paperback – January 2019 by Vex King.*
- *Life's Amazing Secrets: How to Find Balance and Purpose in Your Life | Inspirational Zen book on motivation, self-development & healthy living Paperback –October, 2018 by Gaur Gopal Das.*
- *Thriving Hacks: Simple Hacks For a Richer, Healthier and Fulfilling Life Paperback –October 2021 by Ravikummar M.*
- *Directed by Purpose: How to Focus on Work That Matters, Ignore Distractions and Manage Your Attention over the Long Haul (Six Simple Steps to Success Book 5) Kindle Edition, July,2021 by Michal Stawicki , Anthony Smits.*

REFERENCES

- *The Happiness Tree: Grow Your Happiness by Cultivating a Healthy, Creative and Purposeful Life Paperback – December, 2015 by Shane Eric Mathias.*
- *Who Do You Want to Be? Paperback – May, 2021 by Alina Shahnazari.*
- *The Purpose Driven Life: What on Earth Am I Here For? Paperback –June 2016 by Rick Warren.*
- *Provisions For Your Purpose Kindle Edition, May,2022. by Adetola Balogun.*
- *Purposeful: A Step-by-Step Guide to Finding Clear Direction in a Chaotic World Paperback – September, 2016 by John Carroll.*
- *On Purpose: The Busy Woman's Guide to an Extraordinary Life of Meaning and Success Kindle Edition, October,2021 by Tanya Dalton.*
- *On Purposeful Systems: An Interdisciplinary Analysis of Individual and Social Behavior as a System of Purposeful Events Paperback –July, 2005 by Fred Emery.*
- *Living a Purposeful and Fruitful Life : The 33 Principles Kindle Edition,January,2021. by Michael O. A. Asenso , Nana Amma Oforiwaa Sam.*
- *Incredible Power of Inspiration: Creating the Life You Yearn for Paperback – October, 2017 by Jenifer Zetlan.*
- *Wise Mind Living: Master Your Emotions, Transform Your Life Paperback –January, 2017 by Erin Olivo Ph.D.*

About The Author

Dr. Amit Das, is a renowned executive advisor, consultant, educationist, author, speaker and coach whose 25+ years of business experience provides high-impact, practical solutions that support his clients' leadership development and organisational transformations. Dr. Amit Das is recognised as an innovative, principled thought leader who combines intellectual rigor and discipline with an ability to translate theory into practice. His operational skills are coupled with a strategic ability to analyse, develop, and implement successful strategies for profitability, growth, and sustainability.

Dr. Amit Das has a successful track record in aligning learning and training solutions to key business strategy with a strong focus on flawless execution excellence to facilitate individual, business divisional, and organisational performance. He keeps relentless focus on measuring training impact and ROI, people capability building graphs, training process governance, performance coaching, and strategic thinking. These have been some of his key individual success traits. His core capabilities include performance coaching, designing training and development frameworks, psychometric assessment and analysis, competency framework development and assessments, content design and facilitation of soft skills and leadership programmes, Learning Management Systems, Learning Impact Measurement, Talent Analysis, and Performance Coaching and Counselling.

He has a Ph.D. and a Fellowship in strategic learning, along with his first class degrees in Human Resource Management, Marketing Management, International

Business, and Corporate Laws from the top business schools in India. He is a certified Psychometric analyst, OD Interventionist, Psychologist, Lifecoach, Black Belt (LSS), Strategic Thinker, Talent Analyst, professional coach from the U.K. and behavioral coach from the U.S.A.